SEVEN
SIMPLE
STEPS
to
PERSONAL
FREEDOM

ALSO BY GERRY SPENCE

GERRY SPENCE

SEVEN
SIMPLE
STEPS
to
PERSONAL
FREEDOM

An Owner's Manual for Life

ST. MARTIN'S GRIFFIN
NEW YORK

www.stmartins.com

Library of Congress Cataloging-in-Publication Data

Spence, Gerry.
    Seven simple steps to personal freedom : an owner's manual for life / Gerry Spence.
        p. cm.
    Includes bibliographical references.
    ISBN 0-312-28444-6 (hc)
    ISBN 0-312-30311-4 (pbk)
    1. Free will and determinism. I. Title.

BF621 .S65 2001
123'.5—dc21   2001034893

First St. Martin's Griffin Edition: November 2002

10   9   8   7   6   5   4   3   2   1

To John Dereck,
who was free to the last.

Contents

Note to the Reader

In my journeys across the land, I have observed a universal longing in people. Something is lacking. While many have sought to identify what it might be—not enough money, not enough leisure, not enough education, not enough say in government, not enough medical care, even not enough police protection—my view is that the missing element is freedom. We do not enjoy enough personal freedom to fulfill our vision of the American Dream, our dream.

As I see it, the want of personal freedom is the source of most of the unrest and apathy I encounter wherever I go. Yet no one and no system can deliver personal freedom to us. Slavery in any form begins and ends with the self. If we are to enjoy personal freedom, we cannot look to any state, to any church, to any power other than the power of the self to deliver freedom to us. Still, most of us do not know how to go about acquiring this most precious of life's gifts.

In reviewing my own experience with both slavery and freedom and searching through what I have written about this subject in several books, it seems to me that acquiring personal freedom is something that can, indeed, be taught. My best judgment on the matter is that acquiring it is teachable in simple steps, for my experience also convinces me that the most elusive, the most complicated, indeed, the most vital information that is often held from us on the grounds of impenetrable complexity is, with a minimum of thought and care, usually reducible to a simple formula.

Einstein is said to have written the theory of relativity on a few handwritten pages of yellow notepaper in a form understandable to any high school physics teacher. It is with this thought in mind that I have attempted to present the secrets of achieving personal freedom in an equally uncomplicated way. The result is this little book, *Seven Simple Steps to Personal Freedom*.

Yet it is not my thesis that we can only be freed by revolting against the government, by kissing the workplace goodbye, by telling the boss what we've always wanted to tell him, by abandoning our duties and launching out on our own like some wild beast broken loose from its cage. The ghoul of government, the corporate whipsters, the slave-driving boss, the bank that owns our homes and cars, and the endless responsibilities we have taken on cannot enslave us. That is what this book is about.

I say we are slaves. All of us. And in bewildering ways our bondage is more pernicious than the slavery of old, for we, the New American Slaves, embrace the myth of our freedom like a dead puppy, and with all affection speak to it as if it were alive. Our slave master is the cruelest overseer of all, one who constantly lays the psychic whip to our backs and ensures that we shall remain docile in our shackles and obedient in our chains. That slave master peers over us during all of our waking hours shouting his merciless demands in our frightened ears, intimidating us to work harder, terrorizing us to work longer. He shouts in our faces that should we hold back, should we revolt or attempt to escape, we shall suffer all manner of unmitigated pain, perhaps even death. That slave master who guards us without human compassion, without pity, who drives us unmercifully and threatens us cruelly every day of our lives, is the slave master *within each of us.*

Like slaves on a plantation, we are in this together. And as any heretic, I have an agenda. *I wish us all to be freed.* In forwarding that agenda I have offered seven simple steps leading to our personal freedom—steps that will invest each of us with the power to break out of the zoo. We shall discover how the mind not only constructs the cage but also opens the gate. We shall discover how, experiencing our new liberty, we can never be defeated. And we shall create a new paradigm for success, so that success is based not on the accumulation of wealth and power and status, but on the acquisition of great personhood—a personhood founded on our freedom.

In this small book we shall learn that the inimitable power of the self can free us, that each of us possesses that blessed power, that as we read these words and understand them and take them into ourselves, we own all the perfect power necessary to forever free ourselves.

GERRY SPENCE
Jackson Hole, Wyoming

SEVEN
SIMPLE
STEPS
to
PERSONAL
FREEDOM

My Own Many
Encounters with Slavery

I write out of my own experiences of slavery and share some of them with you so you may judge for yourself the shackles I have worn.

I grew up in a household of slaves. My father was a chemist at a tie plant in the small Wyoming town of Sheridan. He labored at his job faithfully, fearfully, for an all-powerful slave master—the railroad. I remember the irrepressible fear that gnawed at his belly—that in those hard Depression days he might lose his job. We would have to go on relief, and he'd have to work for the WPA, which he saw as the shameful dumping ground for men who were not successful enough to hold a "real job." I remember him incessantly raging to my mother at the supper table about the boss's ignorance, his unfairness to the other workers, and his own sense of helplessness to effectively intervene on their behalf without being cast out. Money was dear. One of his fellow workers died of a ruptured appendix because he wouldn't spend the dollar to see a doctor.

Those were harsh times—six long days of work every week

for $180 a month and not much vacation. Then as now, workers lived in constant fear for their jobs and under the cruel stress of their helplessness to obtain justice in the workplace or fair recognition of their worth. By the time my father was in his early forties, he had lost half his stomach to ulcers. A little more than a decade later, he suffered multiple heart attacks—born, I am convinced, of the endless and cruel frustration of his slavery.

My mother slaved all of her life as a housewife, a slave to the notion that the woman's place was in the home. She grew the garden, canned our winter food, and lived in constant terror that my father might die leaving her and this child of theirs with no support. I remember the insurance salesmen in the living room at night recounting their tales of horror about workingmen we knew who had been killed and about their helpless widows and small children who went hungry. Often my father took large chunks of the wild game he shot for our winter food to some of these piteous women, and my mother took them canned goods from her storage shelves. Out of abject fear my parents bought life insurance that cut deep into the family budget—insurance that many years later when they needed it most wouldn't buy but a couple of days' stay in the hospital.

Next to death and the threat of eternal condemnation, poverty was the most dreadful of human fates. Yet, as poor as we were, my mother insisted that the family tithe, because she was frightened that we might violate any admonition of the Bible. And when my father brought home the few dollars that represented his month's work, 10 percent was faithfully set aside for the church.

I was taught the myths that enslave—that to be successful one must prepare oneself, not to expand the self and explore

2

its magical depths, but to acquire a job. One must obtain an education lest one not be fit to go to work for the slave master—for the railroad like my father; for the government like our next-door neighbor; for someone, yes, please, someone or something that would hire one, take one, and use one so one might live without shame on the face of this earth. Success meant being hired. Success meant being a respected law-abiding wage earner, and climbing the ladder within a hierarchy that had been established by the system. And absolute success meant being at the top of the ladder, looking down from some high perch my father could never achieve. But no one—not my parents, not my teachers, not my friends—ever asked where this ladder was situated.

If one visits the monkey cage in the zoo, one will see the fake tree in the middle of the cage and the monkeys climbing it, swinging from its branches, some sitting at the top picking the lice from their hair and looking down with disdain upon the others below them. As I grew, it never occurred to me that the ladder of success as I understood it might be standing in some impalpable cage that had no visible wire or concrete boundaries, but that was a cage nevertheless.

Faithful to the teaching of my elders and the conventional wisdom of the time, I set out to convert myself into a commodity, one that could be readily sold in the slave market. I had to acquire an education and display a willingness to work hard for others. We, of course, thought ourselves free. We dragged behind us no visible chains. No one lashed at our backs with a visible whip. No one owned a paper showing that they retained title to us. We could not be bought or sold against our will. We could quit the slave master whenever we pleased. We saw ourselves as free to denounce our slavery, but also free, as it were, to starve under the bridge, or to sell ourselves to a new slave master whose demands upon us would prove substantially identical to those made by the master we had left.

The labor market, like the slave market of old, established our value. We would be paid according to the prevailing price for the commodity we had become. In the slave market of old, the slave stood on the auction block naked and ashamed, shivering and terrified while the buyers inspected his body for flaws. Then as now, the market established the slave's worth as it did the worth of a bale of cotton or a bushel of rice.

Today our slavery is less cruel and considerably more subtle. What can the waitress demand in the labor market, the accountant, the engineer with this education and that experience? What is the going price of a computer programmer? What price does a teacher command? In the end we are still seen as mere commodities, and although I do not argue here that we cannot be employed by others and still be free, in certain ways many of us feel as helpless to free ourselves as did the black slave in the cotton fields of old.

We can, of course, launch out on our own. But not unless we can obtain the required financial backing. Money. Where do I get money? I can work for it and save it. That is often a lifetime effort. Many a slave scavenged pennies and borrowed from whoever might lend him a pittance in his attempt to buy his own freedom. One can, according to well-known myth, borrow money from the bank. But only if one has property as security, and only if one is willing to pay the usual usurious interest for its use.

By the time we have paid the interest on our homes—if we are fortunate enough to own one—and the interest on our car and our credit cards, little remains to be mortgaged. Yet, to be sure, some have broken free—but not most. For if most were free of their masters, the economy, dependent on slavery as it is, would collapse. Indeed, today we are as much a slave system as before the Civil War. We struggle only in "a kinder, gentler" brand of slavery.

This is the system in which I was born and educated, the system in which I unwittingly sought with all of my might to be transformed into something that could be sold. Having been born into slavery, I did not know I was a slave, which is the ultimate evil.

That I would someday attend college was a given in my family. From the earliest days that I can remember, I began saving for that day. When my grandmother sent me a crisp dollar bill for my birthday, I was not permitted to spend it. I was marched down to the savings and loan with my little maroon deposit book. There I dutifully pushed the dollar through the cage and in return got nothing back from the lady behind the cage but a penned entry in the book. But all of this was not only proper but blessed, for I was saving for that day when I would go to college and make something of myself—something others might want.

But at the same time, strange and painful things were happening to me that I did not understand. Even at an early age I was beginning to realize that I was not particularly wanted by others. I was not one of those popular boys. I was not taken in as a chum of the upper social set in high school. I was not wanted as an athlete, because I had no special athletic ability. I was not sought after as a leader, because I was somehow different from the others—different in ways I could not define. In a desperate attempt to become acceptable to the high school power set, I tried to be like they were. And when

I was unsuccessful at that, I swaggered a lot, bragged a lot, showed off a lot, made a lot of noise, called attention to myself at every opportunity, all in a futile effort to be seen as special, without realizing that, indeed, like everyone else, I was already special. I felt lonely. The harder I tried to become the someone I was not, the less acceptable I became to those whose acceptance I sought. It was not until many years later that I learned that by attempting to be someone I was not I forfeited what made me special in the first place.

After high school and after a stint in the merchant marine, I finally got to college. By then the money I had saved for college wouldn't have paid the first quarter's tuition. Besides, I gambled it away in the local card room, desperately trying to be somebody. At least somebody with money. But in college I was even less in demand. In those days if you were not a member of a fraternity, you were relegated to a lower caste. When a fellow tried to make a date with a girl, the first thing she would ask was, "With whom are you affiliated?" which was to ask, Do you amount to anything at all? Have you been accepted by those who count on the campus? Do you have a fraternity pin with which to pin me? It was not "Who are you?" but "What badge of acceptance from others do you wear?"

I remember the horrors of "Rush Week." Couldn't one of the dozen fraternities on campus—just one—invite me for a visit—even the lowest fraternity on the social totem? Wouldn't someone please *take me?*

From the beginning I had decided to go to law school, not because I had any idea what it would be like to practice law, but because I couldn't think of anything else to do with my most obvious talent—to stand up and be seen. I could, of course, become a teacher. Or I could become a preacher, which would greatly please my mother. But I thought teachers too poor, and preachers too sissified. And although I had never met a lawyer—didn't even know one—I thought that being a lawyer would probably be just fine; that is, if I could just get a job.

I graduated from law school at age twenty-three. I had already been trained in law school not only to shoulder the harness of hard work but also to be confined by precedent and caged by the tenets of the profession, which were mostly dictated by those in power in order to keep them in power. But one thing I had been told: a lawyer without independent finances must go to work for another lawyer if he is to make a living for himself and his family. By graduation I had already found a nice girl who was not "pin-happy," and married her before she changed her mind, and we had our first child in the crib with a second on the way.

I had graduated cum laude, which, I thought, made me the likeliest person in my class to find someone who would take me; and, as the system promised, I was offered a position— of sorts. An attorney in a small town in the middle of Wyoming offered to provide me with a free office. I would furnish my own typewriter, do my own typing, and he would pay me nothing. But he would direct the overflow from his practice to me. I was ecstatic. Finally I had found someone who would take me. Then I failed the bar exam—the first honor graduate from the University of Wyoming to so disgrace himself and his school.

In those days, failing the bar was as shameful as having been caught in the most blatant of public frauds. Indeed, it meant that I had been a fraud all along and that only now had I finally been caught by the real lawyers—namely, those who administered the Wyoming bar examination. When, six months later, the bar exam was given again, I passed it easily, but by then the lawyer who had offered me the job in the first place thought better of inviting someone so poorly equipped intellectually and educationally as to have once failed the bar. On the day I got notice that I had passed the bar, I set out on my own, going from town to town searching for some lawyer in Wyoming who would please just take me. At last I found a lawyer in the small farming village of Riverton, Wyoming, who must have been more desperate for help than most. He offered me two hundred dollars a month, and I was to do my own typing while he kept all of the fees I generated. I was delighted. Someone having taken me, I was now on the road to success.

But within six months my employer became a judge, and I was forced out on my own. I had this family to support. I looked around. The only path to a job I could find was to run for county and prosecuting attorney. Maybe I could talk the voters into taking me.

I knocked on every door in the several towns in the county, stopped to talk at every farmyard, traveled to the distant ranches in that county, which was as large as some of the smaller states on the Eastern seaboard. I spent days on the Indian reservation "teepee tapping," as seeking votes on the reservation was called in those days. And I was elected.

After that, I worked as a prosecutor for the citizens of the county for two terms—eight years. I was contested in every primary and every general election, and during each I beseeched the voters to take me, for slavery of one kind or another was the only way I knew. By the end of my second term as prosecutor I was still the arrogant show-off, the noisy prosecutor who, for all the show, was still the frightened slave inside. Yet I had done a good job. I had never lost a jury trial as a prosecutor. As I promised, I had shut down the gambling and prostitution houses. I had revoked the liquor licenses of the bars that served minors and violated the Sunday closure laws. I had become the Thomas Dewey of the county, with all the attention attendant upon a budding politician. To be sure, I had made many enemies. Yet perhaps my greatest fear was still the fear I had learned from my parents: What if one morning I awoke to find I was jobless? What if the voters of my county wouldn't elect me again? Once rejected, I would surely perish. And what would become of my family?

Yet some undefined force was pushing me to take even greater risks in order to be taken by an even more important master, this time a statewide contingent of voters. I ran for the U.S. Congress in the Republican primary against William Henry Harrison—not the nineteenth-century president, but that president's incumbent grandson. I carried my own county, and several others, but I lost the election in a landslide for Harrison. The voters of the state would not take me, not over the grandson of a president, even if he did nothing in Congress, never intended to do anything, and had spent most of his life in Indiana. With nowhere to go, with no jobs available, with no one to take me, I was finally forced to take myself. I opened up my private office for the full-time practice of law.

How surprised I was! I soon had many clients. Having learned to try cases as a prosecutor, within a few years I was seen as a fearless fighter who would take on any good fight in court. Shortly the insurance companies that I had regularly beaten began to hire me. I was elated. I thought I had finally made it as a lawyer because lawyers are usually judged by those who own them, and I was now in the employ of numerous large insurance companies. Most big-shot lawyers I knew worked for insurance companies, banks, oil companies, and the railroads, and now I was one of them. It never occurred to me that success had anything to do with the worth of what I did, with justice, or with the honest claims of honest citizens whom I defeated simply because I had the ability to do so.

But something was missing in the equation. By the time I had been in the practice nearly twenty years, I felt empty. Yet I didn't know why. Having never recognized the self as the most unique and valuable gift one can give to one's self, I wanted to be taken by some higher, yet more powerful master who could offer me greater importance than that bestowed on a mere small-town lawyer by insurance companies and other moneyed interests. By this time my family consisted of a faithful wife and four children, and it was time for me to try for something more than representing insurance companies. I would try to get the Wyoming Law School to take me as a professor. And why not?

I remember the day I argued to the dean that I had all of the qualifications for the job: I had been a successful prosecutor. I had defended the accused as well and had never lost a case either as a prosecutor or as a defense attorney. I had set record verdicts in the state for injured persons, and I had represented some of the most important insurance companies in America. I was a cum laude graduate of the university. Certainly I was qualified to teach students trial law. But the dean just laughed.

"No, Gerry," he said. "You wouldn't help our standing at all with the American Bar Association. What we're looking for as a professor is a young graduate from a big Eastern school like Harvard or Yale who has practiced in a big firm somewhere for a year or two. That kind of a man would help our standing." He patted me on the back and showed me the door.

Shortly a vacancy in the judiciary came along in our district. Maybe, I thought, the people would take me as a judge. The district bar association endorsed me—probably thinking it better to isolate me on the bench than to have me thrown against them in the courtroom. But my enemies in the county rose up in multitudes and sent a foot-high pile of letters protesting my candidacy. I remember walking into the governor's office after he had called me to Cheyenne to personally give me the bad news. He would not appoint me to the job.

"Do you see this stack of letters?" he asked. He pointed to the pile on his desk. "These are all protests against you. With this kind of opposition you could never successfully perform the job of a judge in your hometown. Sorry, Gerry," he said, looking sad, and he walked me to the door with his arm around my shoulder.

After that, I decided to give up the law entirely. I was burned-out and disillusioned. I felt trapped. I wanted to be free. I had been a painter for many years, and San Francisco State took me in as a graduate student in their art school. Maybe I could obtain the necessary credentials to become a professor of art. But no. No. Again I didn't fit in. What they were teaching at the art schools in those days seemed shallow, meaningless, empty. And if I didn't readily absorb what they had to offer, they would not keep me.

Entrapped in myself and in a fury of desperation, I moved out of my marriage and out of the community in which I had lived for almost twenty years. In a frenzy I rid myself of nearly every earthly possession I had ever owned right down to the pillows and extra pajamas. I sold my paintings—practically gave them away—sold my home, my little ranch, my rifles, the mounted trophies on the wall. Sold everything. I wanted to be free. Then once more I began the practice of law—this time on the side of those who were injured, damned, and forgotten; those without a voice; those brave human beings often referred to as the little people. Injured and desperate, I began to look to myself. I began the lifelong process of learning who I am. I began to consider what I believed and to ask why I believed it. I began to question myself and to question others as well. I questioned the institutions I had held to be utterly holy. I looked at my prejudices. I took on my fear and saw it as an ever-present, faithful, tormenting friend. And I began to grow.

As I look back, the most fortunate events in my life, although deeply painful, were the rejections I suffered. They proved to be immensely liberating gifts. I shudder to think what would have been my fate had I become a congressman or a professor or a judge. Had any taken me—the voters, the dean, the governor—I would surely have been irretrievably enslaved. Had I been elected to Congress, I would have become enslaved to backroom politicians, to corporate money, and to the fear that one day my decisions might not be pleasing to the voters, without regard to whether or not they might be pleasing to me. One can only imagine the stultifying environment of a law professor in a small Wyoming law school. And imagine the likes of me sitting on the bench as a judge enslaved to the structured life and mentality of the sitting jurist.

All along what I failed to recognize were the forces that had always been at work within. Though I had been born into slavery and taught to follow the rules of a good slave, I had an irresistible longing to be free. Certainly it would be expected that one who had suffered so much rejection during his lifetime might have learned along the way to conform, to make himself more agreeable, to become less offensive, less intimidating, less outspoken, less spontaneous, more predictable, and more structured. I had not yet understood that freedom finally meant I must take myself, accept myself, own myself, be myself, value myself, discover myself, nurture myself, and reject all that violates, imprisons, diminishes, or tends to capture the self. I had not yet learned that, in the end, we are our own slave masters.

During those painful, formative years what I had also failed to understand was that every rejection I had suffered was a true gift of self to me—that no power structure, no entity, no corporation, no constituency, no employer, no person, *no one* and *nothing* could use or value, understand or love me better than I could. What I did not understand was that no authority is empowered to judge me except me, and that no one is entitled to own me or use me except me. What I did not understand was that *taking myself* was the ultimate gift of all, and that that great gift, containing all the other gifts of life, also provided the gift of freedom.

The monkey in the zoo knows the wire of his cage, feels it, slams up against it, and perhaps understands that it is the cage that limits his freedom. Likely he does not blame himself. But when we are held back, when we cannot achieve our erroneous visions of success, most often we blame ourselves for not having worked hard enough, for not having sacrificed enough of ourselves to our employers, for not having possessed sufficient talent or intelligence, for not knowing the right people, for not appearing in the right places, for not belonging to the right country club, for not dressing right or driving the right kind of car. We are enslaved by empty symbols of success that do not acknowledge who we are, that ignore our blessed uniqueness, that trade our incomparable beauty, our spontaneity, our creativity, our passion, and our love in exchange for dead money, worthless goods, and false images of power.

No success is more successful than the successful self, the self that has discovered its unique self, the self that has been freed to possess the self and to burst from the bud of self into the full bloom of self. No power is greater than the power of a self freed of the false ideas of power, for no power exceeds the power of a free self. It answers to no one but the self and serves no one but the self. It can be judged by no one but the self, and seeks to satisfy no one but the self. In so doing, such a self, freed of greed for money and power and all the other false images of success, is able to freely serve others in the unabated fulfillment of the inimitable self.

I do not argue that one can never be free as a wage earner or a government employee, a public servant, a teacher, or a corporate minion. I also do not argue that one can achieve freedom by becoming a professional in private practice or by running one's own business of one kind or another. *Slavery, wherever it exists, is a state of the minda that fails to acknowledge the inherent power of the incomparable self.*

In this system of slavery the crucial questions are simple: Is it possible for us to break free? And if so, how? The answer is that no system, no matter how free; no person, no matter how powerful; no political party, no employer, no parent, no friend—no one can free us except us. We alone can free ourselves. That is what this book is about.

PART I

BREAKING FREE

Recognizing the Slave Within

Man's main task in life is to give birth to himself,
to become what he potentially is.

—ERICH FROMM
from *Man for Himself*, 1947

PERFECT FREEDOM

Perfect freedom does not exist except when we are freed of
life. Then the mind is unprisoned, and the soul is free to fly.
Death frees life, releasing it like a bird that soars without fear
of its enemies, like the sparrow with no fear of the hawk.
Absent death, perfect freedom cannot exist. I do not argue
for death. What I argue for is freedom without regard to the
exterior forces that enslave us. I argue that freedom can exist
only if we have first freed the self. *And in life the self is ours
to free.*

THE FIGHT AGAINST FREEDOM

Most of us do not want to be free. Most of our parents were
slaves. We have grown up as slaves. The system in which we
live and struggle and attempt to fulfill our lives is a system
of slavery. In the end all systems enslave, whether they be
orders of government, religion, or society, and although our

system may offer the best chance for individuals to be free, systems themselves never free us. We must free ourselves.

Once enslaved, few want to burst out from under the leaking roof of the slave hut to freedom and stumble in the cold dark night alone. In the back part of our hearts, we equate freedom with terror. To be free leaves us isolated from the other slaves. Better that we rage until we are palsied, point and squall and wail at fate, shake our fists at God, blame the politicians, blame anybody, everything, because to become free demands that we take responsibility for our bondage. No, we do not want freedom. We were born in slavery. It is too frightening outside the slave hut. We want, instead, *a more comfortable slavery* gilded with bountiful excuses for our servitude.

On the underside of freedom lurks the sense that we are as puny as a particle of dust at sea. We stay imprisoned in bad marriages because we are afraid to be alone. We endure every manner of indignity and outrage, every agony and tedium, because we are afraid—afraid to throw off the traces and experience the naked terror that so dominates the idea of freedom. We kiss our shackles. We stay at home with the old folks, or never leave the farm or the neighborhood. We linger on in daddy's business or hang on to the old job until we have worn a track around it like the knee-deep trail of the old gristmill horse, because we are too frightened to march out into the wilderness alone.

Already we know that no one is ever really free. Not the president, not the chairman of the board, not husband or wife, not the haughty businessman, the playboy, or the idle rich. Freedom is for the birds. And even they are securely bound by their instincts. No. No one is free, and no one wants freedom. We want to talk about it over a beer. To many, freedom is death. If we awakened one day to confront pure freedom, would we not scurry back into our dark little holes as fast as terrorized mice?

Cages are cages whether constructed of steel and concrete or from the fabric of the mind. Like all experiences, both freedom and slavery are registered in the mind. The mind sets the limits of bondage and provides the gate to liberty. What each of us mistakes for our freedom is really our experience within the cage.

I remember when one simply bought one's ticket and hopped on the airplane. Today we have constructed new cages in old zoos. Today we are terrorized by terrorists. Yet there are probably no more than a few score people in the entire nation whose madness would cause them to plot the willful destruction of hundreds of innocent passengers. As a consequence, these few, whoever they might be, control 260 million people. Today we take it as an unquestioned part of travel, as *the way of things,* that we must identify ourselves with an official picture identification—the precursor of tattoos on our wrists. Today we accept as *the way of things* that our bodies must be searched mechanically, that our luggage must be inspected, that once aboard, we must behave in numerous purposeless ways that have little or nothing to do with our safety but control us perfectly like cattle run through the chutes. We know that if someone wants to manufacture a bomb and blow up the plane and its passengers, all of the endless procedures we have endured will have proven to be only the known landscape over which any terrorist can travel with ease.

We do not provide ourselves with safety. We have only given up our constitutional rights against unlawful searches and seizures for the *illusion of safety*. Yet no one complains, or if a complaint is heard, it is in the form of an impotent mumble to which a security guard, who may not be able to read the regulations he has been hired to enforce, responds by warning us to comply at once. Otherwise, we can take the bus to Chicago.

Today one's every move, every decision, every act, is governed by rules and regulations devised, ostensibly, to permit masses of people to function together in harmony. We dress according to rules, eat according to rules, excrete according to rules, sleep according to rules, and die according to rules. We mate according to rules, and, according to rules, we rear and educate our young. To build the simplest house requires compliance with a mountain of rules that would confound all but modern man who has been born into this bureaucratic cage. The rules that govern our daily lives would fill reams of fine print on tissue-thin paper. Still, the human being, more than any other creature, is perfectly able to adapt to nearly any environment. We can swelter and prosper in the jungles. We can tramp over the ice and multiply in igloos. The rules and laws and the multitude of man's endless impositions on man that consume our freedom have become a part of our daily environment to which we have also adapted with little more than an occasional whimper.

The difference, of course, between the monkey in the zoo and the man on the street is that the monkey cannot be contained without physical restraint, while the man can be caged and shackled and whipped and exist in captivity from birth until death within a prison without walls and still believe, at his last breath, that he is free.

FREEDOM INSIDE THE ZOO

Yet we cannot be free outside the cage unless we are able to experience freedom within it. Consider the wild monkey who, lately transported to the zoo, hurls itself against the walls until it is battered and exhausted. Consider how it refuses to eat within the cage and may eventually die. On the other hand, his cage brother, born in the cage, sits peacefully by munching on whatever morsel the zookeeper has tossed him and bounces off the concrete walls as if he were swinging from tree limb to tree limb.

Slavery and captivity are not synonymous for either man or monkey. The wild monkey can be captive in the jungle itself. Relegated to an inferior rung on the monkey-ladder, it is subject to a monkey-imposed hierarchy. In the jungle, it is pinioned to a territory with limits, to the safety of certain trees the leopard cannot climb. In or out of the zoo, the monkey may accept the limits imposed upon him as freedom.

In his preface to *Brave New World*, Aldous Huxley wrote of an army of managers who, without coercion, controlled a population of slaves who were perfectly manageable because they loved their servitude. "To make them love it," he wrote, "is the task assigned in present-day totalitarian states."

HISTORY, OUR SLAVE MASTER

In the same way that nations are the product of their history, so, too, each of us owns a personal history. Just as many nations possess a past in slavery, so, too, each of us has experienced to varying degrees an individual slavery. The deeper we have fallen into slavery, the more difficult it is for us to recognize it, especially if we have been ravaged by its power at an early age. The colt broken to the lead before it has run free is the easier to harness.

THE *ETERNAL NO*

From the moment we are freed from the imprisoning womb and the cord is cut, we not only begin to assert our freedom, to search for it and grasp for it, but at the same moment powerful forces are loosed against us to enslave us. Although we were born to become free, the mother, the community, the law, the system begin to fling the *eternal no* at the child. As the child reaches for a glass on the table, he hears the *eternal no!* He hears "No!" as he toddles toward the door. He hears "No!" as he reaches for the nose on his father's face. He hears the *eternal no* echoing in his ears from cradle to grave. The Ten Commandments, with their "thou shalt nots," ring in his ears. His teachers, more dedicated to their comfort than to the child's free growth and expression, smother the child with the *eternal no* from the first moment he is entrusted into their hands until the factory we call the educational system has, at last, spit him out.

His life is cut into segments of time. The *fence of time* captures him. There is a time to sleep, a time to arise, a time to go to school, to eat, to play, and a time once more to go to bed. Never has the child been permitted to revolt against any of the enslaving forces that domesticate the human animal and convert him from the wild aborigine of his genes to the human machine that will eventually perform as predictably as a windup toy.

THE REBEL WITHIN

By puberty the war between the forces of freedom and those of slavery explodes to the surface. The child, now brimming with hormones, begins to assert his individuality. He strikes out in unpredictable ways against all authority—against his parents, the school, the law. He experiments with alcohol, tobacco, and drugs. He tests his sexuality. No matter the love of parent, the supplications of parent, the pleading of parent, the threats of parent—nothing will divert the child from his rush toward individuality. One cannot experience individuality in the womb, attached to the placenta, suckling at the breast, held by the maternal hand, or contained within the parental folds. Like the slave who breaks his chains, one can achieve individuality only through the rebellious forces of freedom.

But no sooner does the child begin to assert his independence during puberty—although usually with the wisdom and aplomb of a wild hare—than the forces of the *eternal no* are reapplied with even greater vigor. In high school he is no longer coddled. School has become a higher-stakes penitentiary. The rules are impersonal and rigid. The juvenile's own social system, too, has rules. He can belong only if he complies with the gang and accepts its rules. His genetic longing for the tribe shouts in his ear. His need to become a functional, recognized member of the tribe dominates his decisions. To *belong* is the paramount goal. Parental approval and acceptance in the larger social order bear little weight for the adolescent. His is not the adult world, nor does he wish to enter it. He does not respect it. The adult power structure is the enemy. Yet it is from that power structure that the *eternal no* pounds perpetually in his ears—threatening, punishing, and finally enslaving.

ENCOUNTERING THE EVIL BITCH

By the time children blunder into adulthood, other forces have come to assert their power against them. Mother Nature has stricken them with the ultimate disease—falling in love. Her weapon, the evil bitch, is chemical warfare. The hormone, a magic potion still not fully understood by science, strikes at the human brain, causing its victims to fall prey to the disease, to mate, and to thereby plunge into a new slavery from which they will likely never recover. The forces of the malady cause them to woo, to fight, to copulate, and to produce children. Now they must provide their offspring a nest and nourishment, and, in an utterly predictable progression, they must make certain bargains, which usually require them to sell themselves as a commodity at the slave market. Thereafter they make their bargains from year to year, from job to job, and the bargains ensnare them until they are rolled into their graves.

We are creatures enslaved by our genes. We are, indeed, like salmon predictably fulfilling our genetic course. Mindlessly we swim with the school into the great seas and back up the river of our birth to spawn, to die, and to be eaten by the waiting grizzly on the bank. Such freedom as we experience is only that which we encounter within the genetic cage of our birth, within the confines of the mammalian creature that we are—confines from which we can never escape nor, ultimately, wish to escape. We were not born to become free. We were born to fall in love with Mary Jane or Billy Joe, to marry her or him, to parent those three little drippy-nosed rascals who will bedevil us until the day we gasp our last exhausted breath, and then, as true to the equation as dandelions going to seed and withering in the first frost, we, too, will complete this seemingly purposeless cycle established by the ultimate force, which some call God.

THE PESTIFEROUS LONGING

Still we long for freedom. And in the end, we must have it. When the infant's cord is severed, the infant experiences the first power of freedom. It can cry at will. And it does cry, exercising its freedom to protest the external forces already laid against it. The babe can be heard. And it is heard. It can respond to its bodily demands. Already it is an entity to be reckoned with. It has a will of its own. It can exercise its will, and although its dependence is clear to see, its dependence, as in all dependent relationships, enslaves the caretaker as well. Yet freedom is the biological goal of every creature, whether babe or brute. Within the confines of its genes the hawk is free. The squirrel. The worm in the wood. Man is born to struggle for freedom. Yet only man devours the soul of his brother. And only man enslaves others of his kind and himself.

THE FIRST STEP TO FREEDOM: RECOGNIZING THE SLAVE WITHIN

The first halting step toward freedom of the self is the acknowledgment of one's enslavement. If we do not recognize that we are slaves, we can never break free.

We are told that in this American system our destiny rests solely in our hands. But when we slam against the chains of our slavery, we conclude that there must be something inherently wrong with us. Since the rest of the nation is said to be free and enjoy freedom's rich rewards, it must be that we who suffer this powerful sense of insignificance, of aloneness and enslavement, are somehow defective. We must be weak. We must be at fault. We must be worthless.

On the other hand, for those who have been lulled into

the sweet security of bondage, and exist contentedly within the walls of the zoo, for those who embrace myth and splash like happy babies in the bath of blissful conformity, the question naturally arises: Why should they who are content in their servitude be disturbed? Why make happy slaves miserable freemen?

But the destiny of the human race can never be fulfilled under the yoke. The potted plant in the window can never produce its most prodigious blooms. I say God performed the ultimate act of love for Adam and Eve by ejecting them from the Garden, for, confined within the Garden, they existed without the knowledge of freedom, and without suffering its pain the slave can never seek the splendor of the self. *The first step to freedom, therefore, is discovering and freely acknowledging that we are slaves.*

Recapturing the Perfect Self

We are slaves to ourselves. Preserve a closed mind and what we behold is the ambulatory dead. All slaves are a form of the ambulatory dead.

Is it not time to arise from the grave? Is it not time to speak out, to cry out, to fly, to test wings, to fall, and to laugh with joy over the divine bruises?

—GERRY SPENCE
from *Give Me Liberty*, 1998

POWERLESSNESS, THE CONTAGIOUS DISEASE

One night when I was a boy, I was working under the kiln in a cement plant, that hot hellhole where I was shoveling the spill with a guy we called Old Bill. We were talking. I said I was going to become the greatest lawyer in the history of the world. It was just noise, just the sound of my voice against the deafening roar of the kiln, but there was some small entity playing in me—the precocious, naive little fellow called Hope.

"Well, now, that there sounds like a lota bullshit ta me," Old Bill said. "I will tell ya one thing, boy. You be lucky to keep this job, and we'll both get our asses canned if we don't quit fuckin' the dog." He started shoveling harder and faster, and I joined him. "Better get this somebitch cleaned up afore the boss comes by."

We kept on shoveling and sweating. When the wheelbarrow was full, he got between the handles, lifted them up with the hoist of his old legs, and toted the load up over a two-by-twelve plank into the plant proper. After pushing it outside the kiln shed a distance that amounted to a couple of city blocks, he dumped the load where one day a backhoe would lift it into a dump truck to be hauled off. Next load was mine.

When Old Bill got back with the empty wheelbarrow, he jumped right in with his thoughts. "Boy, you best pin yer ass to the grass. You best not go bullshittin' yerself about bein' some big-time lawyer. Them big-time lawyers go to them big schools and wear clean underwear ever day." He laughed. "They ain't our kind. I'll tell ya that much."

I didn't say anything.

"Nothin' wrong with bein' poor. Don't ya ferget that."

Never did. Never have.

"But there is somethin' wrong with bullshittin' yerse'f," he said. "Ya know what the eleventh command is, boy?"

"No," I said.

"The eleventh commandant is "Thou shalt not bullshit thyself." Then it was my turn to lug out the load.

Something there is about feeling powerless that makes us wish the world around us were as powerless as we—something about feeling weak and worthless that causes the human animal to inflict weakness and worthlessness on his fellows. Old Bill, working with a boy under the kiln, saw life as cruel and brutal, and people as worthless and weak. Most often the way folks see others is how they see themselves.

THE PERFECT POWER OF THE SELF

We were born with all the power we require to live free, and all the power we require to free ourselves of life by dying. We need not seek power from others, for others cannot give us power. We need not marry a powerful person, join a political party or club, or wildly climb the corporate ladder to obtain power. To obtain power we do not need to join a church, embrace a religion, adopt its enslaving myths, or mumble its dogma. Each of us has been endowed at birth with the perfect power to be free. No God with whom I would care to carry on an interchange would demand that we submit to him. No loving God would demand our servitude; instead, like any loving father, he would take great joy in our having evolved to a state of independence and would rejoice in our liberation.

The slave master always enlists the power of the slave ghoul. The ghoul knocks at the door of every one of us imploring us to relinquish our power in favor of a state, a religion, an economic philosophy, an employer, a parent, a spouse. The ghoul demands that we give up our power and see ourselves as lowly, powerless and worthless, for without the relinquishment of our power, the slave master is powerless.

THE INCOMPARABLE SELF

I will tell you a laughably simple truth. It is nothing new. It is a truth that has not been invented by any man, or taught by any guru. It is a truth born in the genes of every person. It is as much a part of the person at birth as is his first cry of life. It is as much a part of human history as the thumb is part of a functioning hand. The simple truth is that each of us is *unique* in him- or herself. And because each of us is unique, we cannot be compared to others. Because none of us can be compared to others, we are perfect in ourselves. And because we are perfect in ourselves, we are not required to surrender to any power that is not our own in order to realize our power, our fulfillment, our destiny, our lives.

Think of it this way: Do you see your fingers? Each finger has a print that is different from the print of any other finger. Every person has ten different fingerprints, each of them unique. Every person who has ever occupied space on this earth or who will ever be born until the end of time has ten prints that are each different from those of all others in the history of the world, and in the world to come.

So it is with the imprint of the person. Each of us is different from all other persons living or dead and from any other person who will ever again grace the face of this earth. Such uniqueness renders us incomparable, elevates us as the standard, not for anyone else, but for ourselves—our *only* standard. But it is when the perfect self is relentlessly attacked by the forces of slavery that we become wounded, that we begin to reject ourselves like a malady of the body that turns the immune system against itself. The scars on the soul begin to build and choke until at last we become enslaved to the slave master within.

ATTACKING THE INNOCENT CHILD

I see the perfect child attacked by the evil of the prejudice of those around him. He is black or Hispanic, or poor or small. She is shy, or her body does not fit the anorexic paradigm of the New York City cover girl. And the child takes the judgment of others into him- or herself.

I see the perfect children of the world injured by racism, by poverty, and by the stultifying forces of ignorance. I see children stuck in the ugly mire of communities where crime is the norm and poverty the standard. And the child with no vision other than lawlessness and destitution accepts the judgment of the system as a valid judgment of himself. The system has abandoned the child's community. In the child's innocent mind, those within the community must therefore be worthless. Human life must be worthless, including his own, so that injuring and killing at last become meaningless acts in an empty world.

I see the creative genius in our children—that budding flower that stands for the incomparable power of the human species—being debased and corrupted by fathers who feel worthless and powerless themselves and who, in turn, visit their dreadful disease of dysfunction and slavery upon their children. I see parents telling their children that they are bad, that they are ignorant and stupid, and the judgment of the parents is taken as the truth by the child. I see parents who prove the worthlessness of the child to the child by ignoring his or her uniqueness, by disregarding the child's beauty, and by abdicating the care of the child to those who have no investment in the child—the corporate nanny, the day-care center, the impersonal overseer. I see parents abusing children, both with words and with physical force that communicate the irrevocable message to the child that he or she has no value, for otherwise the child would be treated with endearing respect.

REJECTING THE PERFECT PERSON

With deep grief I see perfect people who have become absorbed in the blinding fervor of a rigid political philosophy, in the inflexible dogma of both spiritual and economic religions, in ideas and beliefs and myths that denounce the perfect person and, at last, cast him into slavery. For the slave is only the slave so long as he sees himself as more valuable as an item of trade than as a growing person of beauty. The slave is only the slave so long as he sees himself as imperfect. The slave can be a slave only when his perfect uniqueness is denied—denied by him for himself. Only then can the otherwise perfect person become transformed into a thing, into a commodity that, like any slave, stands for sale.

TAKING BACK THE GIFT OF THE SELF

The gift of the self cannot be given to us. It is the incomparable gift that has already been given. We have possessed it from the beginning. Ours is the gift of our perfect uniqueness that cannot be purchased by buying a new car, by wearing designer clothes, by appearing in the "right" crowds, by joining the "right" clubs, or speaking or thinking in the "right" way. The gift cannot be given to us by money or by things. The gift cannot come to us by our domination and enslaving of others. The gift cannot come to us from outside ourselves. The gift was already given and thereafter stolen from us by the forces of slavery.

Having understood this simple truth, the gift can be taken back—simply—*like that!*—like turning on the light, the blessed light.

THE SECOND STEP TO FREEDOM:
RECAPTURING THE PERFECT SELF

The second step to personal freedom is therefore acknowledging as an irrefutable fact our uniqueness, and therefore our perfection. We are perfect as the Hope diamond is perfect. There is no one to whom we may be compared—no one in the universe—no one now, no one in the past, no one to the end of time. Our absolute acceptance of that truth—and it is a truth—is our most powerful step to freedom. Yet our view of ourselves as perfect, accurate as it is, is not one of conceit but one of inclusion because we realize that all others in this world contain their own uniqueness and therefore their own perfection as well.

And because you are perfect, you respect yourself and others in new ways. You find yourself at war with old ideas about yourself. You begin to understand that what you saw as your deficiencies before are in reality the unique prints of your personhood—that each of your traits in whatever quantity—your intelligence, your physical makeup, your temperament, your passions and emotions—are components that make up who you are. They are the ingredients in your personal recipe. You begin to realize that each of us is made up of different ingredients in infinitely varying amounts and that the product for each is as different as the desert landscape is different from the forest. Yet both the desert and the forest are perfect, just as you are.

Having discovered your perfect self, embraced your perfect self, and accepted your perfection as irrefutable, you can begin to free yourself of the crippling judgments and the injurious assaults that have falsely labeled and cruelly disabled you. Realizing your perfection places you in a different mental landscape. No longer are you required to engage in vain imitations of others. No longer do you covet their perfection. Instead, you begin to uncover the ever-expanding borders of your own uniqueness, your unlimited hidden talents, your undiscovered passions, indeed, your incomparable self, which distinguishes you from every other creature living or dead.

You begin to realize the primal roots of all slavery—that slavery is imposed on those who compare themselves with others. Slavery begins with the false sense that we are less intelligent than others without understanding that true intelligence cannot be measured with the structured exams and fabricated tests of the psychologist. Slavery begins when we erroneously judge that we are not as beautiful as others without understanding that beauty cannot be measured by any model or compared according to any standard. Slavery begins with the false idea that our worth is measurable by the money we earn or the beliefs we embrace. Soon you begin to understand that slavery is inflicted upon those who have abdicated their limitless power to others—a power that has been turned against them and that enslaves them. Indeed, you begin to understand that the perfect self can never be enslaved—not in the workplace, not at home, not in the bedroom, and not in the world at large. The perfect self was born perfect. And the *reborn* perfect self, also, shall soon be free.

Inquisitor of the Self

*No, when the fight begins within himself, a man's
worth something.*

—ROBERT BROWNING
from *Bishop Blougram's Apology*, 1855

BECOMING THE RELENTLESS QUESTIONER

Like the child realizing he is locked in the basement, we begin
to explore for a way out. *Having acknowledged our servitude,* we are freed to test new ideas, to test what is said to
be right and what is said to be wrong, to test religion, to test
the rules, the rhetoric, the declarations of freedom—in the
end, to test all authority including our own. Ah, to test authority, every strand and thread of it that entwines us! To
test the authority of government, of the law, of the enveloping
system—yes, even to test our perception of the universe. *I
say, test it all.* As Lord Byron said, "If I am a fool, at least I
am a doubting one."

I say, test all inner authority as well. Test the loudmouthed
tyrant called conscience, that inner voice that shouts and nags
and wails, that orders us to perform what it defines as duty.
I say, grab the inner despot by the throat. Call it up to answer. By what authority does it command us to accept a religion, to bow to an icon, to salute a piece of cloth, to perform

services we detest or disrespect, to fulfill the expectations of parents and children and those who prevail upon us and suck our lives from us under the guise of friendship? By what authority does it command us not to deviate—not one whit— not to try new behavior or stray one step from the rutted path? We must make demands of our own and hurl the question back. For the shackles are slipped over us while we, the compliant, stand as silent as stones. Silence gags us in the dark and chains us like the slave to the whipping post.

Freedom is always at war with the opposing forces of slavery. Always. Freedom to think, to explore, ah, to *wonder,* is at war with snarling religions that command that we not think, not explore, and accept on faith whatever is flopped before us on the plate of life. Freedom to experiment, to try the new, to reach out, to look over the abyss, is at war with the demands of the system that we slink up to the master and, like good slaves, fulfill his expectations. The penalty for being who we are, and, therefore, for being different, is to face the deep and intense fear of being banished from the tribe.

Freedom itself is at war with the myths of freedom. Being told we are free, being educated to see ourselves as free agents, being conditioned to believe that freedom is ours because we were born in "a free country"—all these processes rely on myth. The myths of freedom blind us like fog settling in over the front porch. And only by exposing the myths that surround us can we hope to regain our liberty.

BELIEF, THE INVISIBLE SHACKLE

One needs to begin by taking an inventory of the *self*. What is this conglomeration of beliefs, likes, prejudices, habits, customs, and thought processes that make up the *self*? I say, examine these beliefs. *Test them*. Take each into the fingers of the mind like someone examining an egg for cracks. Turn each over and over again. Does such a belief or prejudice close the doors to experience? A belief is dangerous to embrace. We have become slaves to beliefs, to points of view that leave us with locked-tight, jammed-shut minds and imprison us to petty habits. We are slaves to our hatreds, our prejudices, to our miserly view of our own worth and the worth of our neighbors. We are slaves to enslaving values, which are usually set not by ourselves but by others.

The most formidable chains are forged from beliefs. Ah, beliefs! Beliefs tear out the eyes and leave us blind and groping in the dark. If I believe in one proposition, I have become locked behind the door of that belief, and all the other doors to learning and to freedom, although standing open and waiting for me to enter, are now closed to me. If I believe in one God, one religion, yes, if I believe in God at all, if I have closed my mind to magic, to spirit, to salvation, to the unknown dimensions that exist in the firmament, I have plunged my mind into slavery. *Test all beliefs. Distrust all beliefs.*

We are animals who travel the same trails in the forest every day. If that were not so, there would be no trails in the forest. We get up in the morning and proceed through the same routine every day. We turn on the coffeepot, let out the dog, stagger to the shower, brush our teeth, blow our hair dry, let the dog in, and pour our second cup of coffee. If anything intrudes into the routine, the intrusions bring on immediate irritation. Every day we drive to work over the same route, have lunch at the same place, often with the same people, and, in sum, encounter the same daily routine that has already left us mindless and benumbed. At last we fall into bed to watch the same inane sitcoms on television, which will paralyze the few remaining brain waves that dare slither across the mind's blurry screen.

When we proceed through one day in one way, for sure we have experienced that day. If we repeat the same routine on the second day, we have still lived but one day—the first. Some people have spent a lifetime engaged in the monotonous repetition of that first day, day after day, and at last they die having lived little more than that one monotonous day of their lives. Routine, habit, and fear of something new have become the venal thieves of freedom. *Test your habits. Abandon those that reduce you to the slavery of sameness.*

Most of us are enslaved by the economic or social class in which we exist. Rarely does the wealthy man have lunch with the plumber. I know black men and white men who have worked together in harmony every day until their retirement but who have never enriched themselves by having had dinner together along with their families. Often the self-professed intellectual has never tried to discover the intelligence of the truck driver, who holds insights not discoverable in books. The psychologist who counsels people every day in accordance with the procedures he learned in school has never talked to an Indian shaman about man's relatedness to Mother Earth, or to the street-corner guru concerning the state of the species. The physician whose view of himself as godlike and which sometimes leaves him pathetically ignorant, has never talked to a Chinese herbalist, and knows little of any medication that has not first been explained to him by the marketers from the drug companies.

Most of us are trapped—trapped by our education and trapped by the minutiae of our experience. Although the freed self is the source of all knowledge, most of us are imprisoned in a false sense of self, the authority for which is often little more than transplanted prejudice and half-truth. Nothing serves us so handily, so frequently, and so well as blithe ignorance. Our system of likes and dislikes, which renders us as predictable as the clock that strikes on the hour, reduces us to machinery—machinery waiting to be manipulated, turned on, turned off, used up, or wasted according to the need of the master. *Test your likes, and view with suspicion your dislikes.*

THE QUESTION—THE WEAPON THAT FREES

Testing, questioning, is the great weapon against slavery. By what right do parents, teachers, professors, the media, the government program, the church dictate to us? Question every word, every phrase of every alleged truth that is fed to you. Strip every myth naked to its rattling bones. Propaganda and myth are the evil potions that are administered to us by the witch doctors of the system, and that anesthetize our minds and leave us limp and lifeless on the system's operating table. Skepticism, not cleanliness, is next to godliness. Skepticism is the father of freedom. It is like the pry that holds open the door for truth to slip in. Authority cannot bear the glare of the question. Question every truth, for what is true for the master is rarely true for the slave. *I say, test it. Question it, demand that it answer. Then test the answers.*

THE INQUISITOR OF THE SELF

And the self? Can the self be the receptacle of truth? *I say, question the self.* Become the relentless inquisitor of the self. Are not the ideas that cling to the walls of the self like barnacles on the ship's hull—the dictates of parent, of church, of religion, of politics? Question every prejudice. Ask, whom do my prejudices and my beliefs serve? If we are prejudiced in favor of an economic theory and blindly believe in its virtues, our prejudice may well be serving the master. If we are prejudiced against a race, our prejudice likely serves the rich against the poor. If we blindly believe in the justice of a system, or the fairness of a political philosophy, our beliefs when tested will rarely serve us.

When, by prejudice, we separate ourselves from other members of the species, our sense of brotherhood is diminished. Such alienation always serves the few who, by dividing and separating us from each other, conquer and devour us. Think of the fate of the wolf if a thousand sheep in the herd, in unison and in deep caring for themselves and each other, descend upon the wolf with four thousand stamping hoofs.

THE BROTHERS — FEAR AND FREEDOM

Still, when, upon the authority of the self, we conclude that we must leave the pack, we are terrified at the thought of standing alone, for we are vulnerable. Listen to the words of the nineteenth-century philosopher Nietzsche:

> Do you have courage, Oh, my brothers? Are you brave? Not courage before witnesses but the courage of hermits and eagles, which is no longer watched even by a God. Cold souls, mules, the blind, and the drunken I do not call brave. Brave is he who knows fear but conquers fear, who sees the abyss, but with pride. Who sees the abyss but with the eyes of the eagle; who grasps the abyss with the talons of the eagle—that man has courage.

And that man is free. Fear and freedom are warring brothers. I know of no act of courage that is not accompanied by fear, for courage cannot exist without fear.

THE YOKE OF POLITICAL CORRECTNESS

Today most of us are starched up stiff in the high, white collar of political correctness. What is deemed politically correct is as likely to enslave us as are our prejudices. Are we not prohibited by political correctness from freely discussing what distinguishes man from woman, black from white, Jew from gentile? We are not all alike, but we are no longer permitted to celebrate our differences. Political correctness functions to silence us. It eliminates our right to ponder the issues important to our lives and to think for ourselves. In an allegedly free society it has become society's censor. It separates us from each other, for if I cannot express myself to you lest what I say be politically incorrect, you cannot respond to me in such a way that I may learn from you. Political correctness is the hollow voice of power exhorting the slaves to let the master think for them. It is often no more than the dictates of a group of self-appointed censors foisting their doctrine on us. *I say, question relentlessly, bravely, that dogma that is said to be politically correct.*

THE THIRD STEP TO FREEDOM:
TO TEST AND TO QUESTION

The third step to freedom is to test and to question. That we have always assumed an idea to be true, a premise to be sound, an assumption to be reliable, a commandment to be incontestable, a law to be just, a feeling of patriotism to be legitimate, a like or dislike to be well-founded is dangerous: Every idea, belief, and position we take for ourselves must always be tested.

The question to ask is, why do I believe this? The question to ask is, would I have believed this had I been born in a different country, if my parents had belonged to a different church, or if I had been taught a different set of values? How much are my beliefs, my likes, or my dislikes founded on teaching by others—doctrine that has been foisted on me from the time I was an innocent child rather than what I have discovered for myself?

Testing, questioning, is as becoming a child again. It is the way of innocence, of rebirth, and, at last, of wisdom. It permits us to return to that exciting adventure of rediscovering ourselves as well as the world around us. The mind sets the boundaries to the cage, but the mind can also fling open the doors to permit the spirit caged within to once more roam free.

Becoming Religiously Irreligious

*Question with boldness even the existence of God;
because if there be one, He must approve the homage of Reason rather than that of blindfolded Fear.*

—THOMAS JEFFERSON
from a letter, 10 August 1787

REJECTING THE SLAVE MASTER WITHIN

When I speak of religion, I mean an institutionalized system of belief that is taken on faith and obeyed. By this definition we suffer many religions: religions of church, of state, and of the various economic and political systems that wield power in the world. Lifestyles and value systems themselves are often religious in nature.

The fourth step to freedom is to become irreligious. I say, go to war against religion—not against the religion of others, but against those metabolized religions of the self that you have been force-fed and that, once absorbed into the psyche, poison the self like an evil potion. "Religion," said Carl Jung, "is for people who want to avoid the experience of God." I say religion is for people who want to avoid the experience of the self.

When I say we should throw off our religions, I am not suggesting we abandon our moral foundations. The distinction of right from wrong does not depend upon religious be-lief. The so-called godly man may be more likely to do serious wrong than a man who deeply questions himself. The "godly man" often zealously follows religious precepts that, in the end, justify an unjust injury to others, while the questioning man, addressing his own conscience, may have the better chance to consider all the circumstances and come to the just decision.

A few centuries ago, if we questioned the commands of the church, indeed, if the church, as inquisitor, found that we were guilty of heresy, we might be skinned alive, stretched on the rack, disemboweled, or burned at the stake. Today, as the God-appointed arbiter of all morality, the church still inserts itself into the personal lives of its true believers, making de-cisions for the individual concerning issues that extend from the first act of procreation to the last breath of dying. And should we think or act for ourselves, the church may still torture us with the pain of guilt, the fear of excommunication, or the threat of eternal condemnation.

To conclude that by rigid rule only the church can deter-mine right from wrong is to admit—as, indeed, the church insists we should—that man is born in sin and is fundamen-tally evil. To conclude that only the church is capable of de-termining right conduct from wrong is to rob man of the dignity of a personal conscience in favor of the conscience of an institution. I have never known an institution with a con-science, be it a club, a church, or a state. Institutions impose rules and laws. People have consciences. I say rules and laws have always been poor substitutes for the conscience of a fully evolved human being.

Religions are the means by which those who "run the club"

obtain power over the masses. So far as the church is concerned, we are told we must relinquish our power to God, and, in return, through prayer beseech God to give us back our power. The message is that alone, and without the direction of pope, priest, or scripture, we are too measly and too niggling to experience God. I am not arguing that we should abandon our communication with any god in whatever form we may envision, be that god a white man with a long white beard, a black woman with her boundless nurturing power, or the universe itself with its infinite questions and infinitely elusive answers. I argue only that the creation of a personal god, if any, or the rejection of God, if complete, is a matter of individual choice that should be freely exercised without the dictates of any church and without the commands of any state.

To the same extent that hearts, livers, and kidneys can be transplanted from one human being to another, so, too, religions of every sort can be superimposed upon the mind. Indeed, the transplanting of a heart may extend the life of the recipient. But the transplanting of a set of religious beliefs onto the psyche of a person serves only to limit his life. In the end, religions preclude the individual from writing his own life's script, which is the single most marvelous gift that life ever offers.

A nearly universal truth is that religions are in the service of the master rather than the slave. Religions extract the inherent power of the person and concentrate such ill-gotten power in the church or the state, thereby rendering the power-taker as omnipotent and the power-giver utterly weak. When Marx condemned religion and the church, he was simply overthrowing an old religion in favor of a new one—his. The new religion was, of course, called Communism. If I take

Communism as my personal religion, I worship a state-owned system of production and distribution of goods and abdicate my right of personal choice to the dictatorship of the proletariat. On the other hand, capitalism is equally a tyrant. If I take capitalism as my personal religion, the market may become God even though people may be starving or the environment devastated. That people become the mere fodder of religions cannot be better illustrated than by the ghastly fact that both of these warring economic religions were willing to destroy every human being on the face of the planet in a nuclear holocaust in the name of the religion each system espoused.

Under any religion, the preestablished impersonal code transcends the right of the individual to explore, experience, and marvel at the mysteries of his own life and death. Religions introduce us not to God but to slavery. They deprive us of our freedom to explore our own souls and to discover the endless and wondrous possibilities presented to us by an infinite universe. And most often the method of religions is fear, not love. They demand blind obedience and often obedience to dreadful dogma. Most often one is taught that if one permits one's thoughts or acts to stray from the Scriptures, whether the Scriptures be those of Christ or Mohammed, of Marx or Adam Smith, one shall be severely punished.

If one violates the ordinances of state or church, even when such a power-taker is wrong, one may be dealt with as a criminal, a deserter, a traitor, or a heretic. In our own times we remember how many of our loyal citizens were destroyed as "Reds" during the infamous days of McCarthy, and how protestors against the Viet Nam War were reviled, persecuted, and expatriated as "un-American," some of whom have never recovered. Religions rarely make room for the independent ethical judgments of the individual. Such judgments, like a ready-made suit of clothing, have been prefabricated for the person whether the suit fits or not.

According to the church we were born damned by the sins of Adam. Is sin inheritable? Is damnation bequeathed from generation to generation like part of the genetic pool? What foolishness, what malignant stuff religion is that it teaches once-perfect children to grow up caulked with inherited guilt over an antediluvian's alleged intercourse of one kind or another with a snake! And over an apple? The fear of religion—the sometimes grand dementia of it!

The wild-eyed at the corners who rage from their soap-boxes and proclaim themselves to be Christ are no more mad and much less dangerous than the religious zealots who teach that the overpopulation of the earth, which may inevitably result in the demise of the species, is a matter in which Christians have no responsibility whatever—that only the love of God is their responsibility. The fetus is their responsibility, but the starving children of the world are not. Such madness is taught, not caught. It is not the product of diseased minds, but of healthy minds that have been injected with the malady of religion. If, therefore, the definition of insanity is a state of mind that renders a person incapable of distinguishing reality from delusion, must we not acknowledge that, through religion, insanity can also be taught?

In the end, nothing is more enslaving than a mind choked by the tentacles of intolerant dogma. The birds, provided with wings, are permitted to fly. The fish, provided with fins, are permitted to swim. Should the antelope fold up its racing legs and the bee cease making honey? The door to enlightenment is the mind. The door to freedom is also the mind. Having provided the door, would God command that the door remain locked?

RELIGION AND THE SLAVE

Yet, as we shall see, religion itself has always been the servant of those in power. In 1859, the Agriculture Society of Union District, South Carolina, made a study to determine the bearing of religion on the productivity of their slaves. The published report concluded that it was "the best policy and the highest interest of the master to afford good religious instruction to his servants." *Religion pays,* and, as the report pronounced, it "aids greatly in the government and discipline of the slave population." The report recommended the employment of religious instructors, even at considerable cost. "The investment is not as great as the actual dividend in way of improvement." The report went on to cite such benefits to the master as "a stronger sense of duty upon the part of the Negroes to obey," and "a feeling of fear to offend against the obligations of religion."

Yet one planter, a year later, wrote to his fellow slave-holders:

I do not think—with sorrow I pen it—that [the Negro slave] is capable of moral elevation to any very appreciable extent. . . . [I believe that] an inscrutable Providence will eventually work out his moral elevation, through the agency of the white man I have not a doubt; but it must be done by "moral suasion," coupled with a smart sprinkling of that great civilizer—the cow hide.

From the earliest times man has used God as his authority to enslave his fellow man. One planter wrote in his advice to fellow planters:

Let us remember that it [slavery] is an institution ordained of Heaven, and that we are the chosen instruments for the melioration and civilization of the downtrodden and oppressed African race. Placed in this position by Providence, we should feel and appreciate the responsibility and importance of our station, and so discharge our duties as to fulfill Heaven's designs toward us.

To the slave, the master's religiosity became the ultimate evil. Frederick Douglass wrote to his former master:

When I saw the slave-driver whip a slave woman, cut the blood out of her neck, and heard her piteous cries, I went away into the corner of the fence, wept and pondered over the mystery. I had some idea of God, the Creator of all mankind, the black and the white, and that he had made the blacks to serve the whites as slaves. How could he do this and be *good*, I could not tell. I was not satisfied with this theory, which made God responsible for slavery, for it pained me greatly, and I have wept over it long and often.

Susan Boggs, a black runaway interviewed in Canada in 1863, said of the religious slave masters:

Why the man that baptized me had a colored woman tied up in his yard to whip when he got home that very

Sunday and her mother . . . was in church hearing him preach. He preached, "You must obey your masters and be good servants." That is the greater part of the sermon, when they preach to colored folks. . . .

SLAVERY AND THE CHURCH

Indeed, the church itself has often condoned slavery. In 1610 Father Sandoval of Spain wanted to know the position of the church on slavery and inquired of the matter to a monk. Here was the reply:

I think your Reverence should have no scruples on this point. . . . We have been here ourselves for forty years and there have been among us very learned Fathers. . . . Never did they consider the trade as illicit. Therefore we and the Fathers of Brazil buy these slaves for our service without any scruple.

The church owned many slaves. Even before the Jesuits began to import Africans to the New World, the church was active in its promotion of slavery. Pope Gregory XI thought slavery was justice for those who had struggled against the papacy, and ordered the enslavement of excommunicated Florentines whenever they were captured. In 1488 Pope Innocent VIII accepted a gift of a hundred Moorish slaves from King Ferdinand of Spain, and divided them up among the various cardinals and nobles.

St. Augustine himself pronounced that "the chief cause of slavery, then, is sin . . . and this happens only by the judgment of God, in whose eyes it is no crime." Pope Pius XII, although aware of the Nazi concentration camps, turned a blind eye, and the Vatican is said to have facilitated the escape of more

Nazis after World War II than any other government or institution.

GOD AND THE SLAVES OF THE NORTH

The view of the religious zealot so prevalent in the Old South was equally at work in the industrial North, where slavery took on only a slightly different form. In 1902 George Baer, the president of the Philadelphia and Reading Railroad, who spoke on behalf of the coal operators, answered the striking coal miners who begged for Christian treatment. "The rights and interests of the laboring man," he announced out of the pits of his sanctimoniousness, "will be protected and cared for—not by the labor agitators, but by the Christian men to whom God, in His infinite wisdom, has given the control of the property interests of this country." Usually the miners were dead by forty—if not from escaping gasses and the caving roofs of the mines, then from lung disease. They worked six days a week, sometimes seven, and often labored fourteen straight hours below the surface of the earth.

Within a short time, at Ludlow, Colorado, the striking workers' tent settlements at John D. Rockefeller's Colorado Fuel and Iron Company were burned to the ground, and the occupants, including women and children, were burned and shot, not by raiding Indians but by Rockefeller's private army backed up by the U.S. Cavalry. Rockefeller, a worshipful, some claimed a God-fearing man, had himself been captured by the religion of the dollar, which put his love of wealth and power over his caring for living persons—his workers—whom he ultimately sacrificed for profit. Rockefeller was said to have monitored the miners' struggle at Ludlow with great pleasure.

One miner, William Snyder, was called as a witness to the

coroner's inquest over the death of his eleven-year-old son, who had been shot through the head:

"They set fire to the tent?" Snyder was asked.

"Yes, sir," he replied. "My wife then said, 'For God sakes save my children.' "

"What did they say to you?" the coroner asked. Snyder replied:

> They said, "What the hell are you doing here?" I told them I was trying to save my children and they said, "You son of a bitch, get out of here and get out quick at that."
>
> My wife was out by that time. . . . I told them to hold on. I had a boy killed in there and they told me to get out damn quick. I picked the boy up and laid him down outside so I could get a better hold of him. I asked some of these fellows to help me carry him to the depot and one said, "God damn you, aren't you big enough?" I said, "I can't do it." I took him on my shoulder and [lifted his] sister on the other arm and then one of these militia men stopped me and said, "God damn you, you redneck son of a bitch, I have a notion to kill you right now."

In the South, during the Civil War the church was, as is its wont, aligned with power. Archbishop John Hughes declared: "We Catholics, and a vast majority of our brave troops in the field, have not the slightest idea of carrying on a war that costs so much blood and treasure just to gratify a clique of Abolitionists." The abolitionists themselves seemed blind to the nearly complete enslavement of hundreds of thousands of white children by the industrial North in its own sweatshops.

After the Civil War, free enterprise became the dominant religion of the industrial North. That religion also served the master, and, as always, the master required an endless supply of workers who would sell their labor cheap—workers who could be manipulated to all but give their lives away. Henry Ford proclaimed that "work is the salvation of the nation." Indeed, Henry Ford saw his workers as little more than fungible supplies. He thought that "a great business is really too big to be human." He preached to his workers:

> If you are a high-priced man you will do exactly as this man [the foreman] tells you, from morning 'til night. When he tells you to pick up a pig and walk, you pick it up and walk, and when he tells you to sit down and rest, you sit down. You do that right straight through the day. And what's more, no back talk.

Ford, who was considered by his employees as an absolute tyrant, told a journalist, "I have a thousand men who, if I say, 'Be at the northeast corner of the building at four A.M.,' will be there at four A.M. That's what we want, *obedience*." It made no difference that the new slaves were wage slaves. Slaves were slaves. In its multifarious forms, religion over the centuries has served the master well, admonishing the worker that he can row himself to heaven only up a river of honest sweat.

Today, the church, in its endemic attraction to power, lends its blessing to the unfettered exploitation of the American worker by the corporate power structure, and American industry, without a flinch of conscience, and following the gospel of free enterprise, uses up the impoverished workers and their children in the Third World like so much coal to fire the money boilers. To put some perspective to it, Michael Jordan has been paid more for his endorsement of Nike shoes than all of the laborers in the Third World, some of them children, have been paid to manufacture the shoes he promotes.

THE MAGICAL DIMENSION OF SPIRITUALITY

I do not reject the magical dimension of spirituality. I leave open the possibilities of whatever grace the human mind can imagine. I cherish the fantasy, even the hope, of adventures in other realms to come. But how can we choke out that most precious of all gifts, life, with the rope of religion around our necks? It chokes out freedom with dogma. It pinions us to the stake of superstition. It binds us with fear to a system in which the masters themselves have become the obedient slaves of Mammon.

THE RELIGION OF FREE ENTERPRISE

The religion of free enterprise preaches that it is acceptable, even laudable, to destroy the earth and to starve its population in pursuit of profit. It is a religion that worships *things* more than it cares for people, a religion in which wealth in gold is more cherished than wealth in human worth.

The religion of free enterprise promises deliverance in exchange for submission. It returns us to the Garden, but the Garden is molded of concrete and perfumed with the smoke of industry. In this garden, those once bonded to the beauty of the earth must join in its systematic destruction. In the

Garden one cannot hear the angels sing. In the Garden one hears only the endless moaning of workers laboring for material things.

THE RELIGION OF PATRIOTISM

I am not against loyalty to a system that shows loyalty to its members by respecting every individual's personal freedom of choice. But blind patriotism is yet another form of religion that often enslaves the people for the benefit of the master. Do we not understand by now that blind patriotism is not always good for the health of the people—the stirring, patriotic rhetoric, the flags unfurling, the bands marching, the people charging off to war? Do we not understand by now that the message of patriotism is often an invitation for the people to serve the system rather than for the system to serve the people?

All "isms" become religions. The Nazi party, the Communist party, the notion of the sacredness of capitalism, indeed, of any "ism," any economic theory, any government that demands the submission of the individual to the interests of the state, is an invitation to slavery.

FREEING OURSELVES FROM THE
RELIGION OF CONFORMITY

We are so bound by the various religions of our culture that we scarcely recognize their power over us. Social niceties are often religiously adhered to—small things that reflect the abdication of sovereignty over the self. Even if one is hungry, one does not ask for soup while the others at the table are giving the waitress their drink orders. If one goes to the Met, one does not attend in jeans even if the comfort would lend to the evening's enjoyment. One stops at the stoplight waiting for it to turn green even if it is four in the morning and not a soul occupies the streets in any direction for miles around. One faithfully bows one's head and closes one's eyes during public prayer whether or not one is praying, and one salutes the flag as it passes whether or not the flag at the moment symbolizes the moral and respectable stance of the nation.

Conformity can become religious in nature. Too often we do not speak out when someone in our presence is guilty of a racial slur. Nor do we walk away from cruel jokes that belittle ethnic origins or sexual preferences. The religion of conformity is comfortable. It does not require us to think or act ethically. Often we accept the party line in times of illegal wars, unjust acts of Congress, and the immoral proclamations of our leaders. We are saved always by the religion of conformity and, on the other hand, fear banishment from the tribe should we exercise independent thought or engage in dissent.

I say that every day we should try to violate some rule, some standard code of conduct, even some senseless law, as an exercise against the dominance of the religion of conformity. I say we should exercise our independence against the religion of conformity in the same way that we exercise our bodies.

I am not arguing that we should become common criminals, nor do I urge the abandonment of common courtesies. I argue, instead, that we should ask ourselves why we do what we do. Why do we call a judge "Your Honor" when he may be dishonorable to the core, or address a preacher as "Reverend" when he may be utterly irreverent concerning the rights of the individual? Why do we bow and scrape to the extremely wealthy when, indeed, they may be only extremely greedy? Why do we seek the autograph of certain celebrities when they may be rascals of the worst sort and when, at the same time, we wouldn't think of asking for the autograph of a mother who has raised ten children by herself and put them through college without help?

THE PREEMINENCE OF RELIGION OVER MAN

To the religious, whether their religion is one of God or money or politics, it is the religion itself that counts. Religion, the product of man, is not responsible to man. It is responsible only to itself. It has no duty to free the lives of men. It has only the duty to capture them. It has no duty to elevate them. It has only the duty to frighten them, to cut off inquiry, to block their discovery of the self, and at last to use and to own them. Religion has too often become the debasing negative energy that demands that we praise religion and denigrate the person.

I say religion is not "the opiate of the people," as Marx declared. I say that religion is the stake to which the slave master within pickets the mind as the goatherd tethers his goat.

THE RELIGION OF WORK

The British Labor politician Bruce Grocott once said, "I have long been of the opinion that if work were such a splendid thing the rich would have kept more of it for themselves." What of the religion of work, that deep, neurotic worship that proclaims work in itself as the ultimate virtue? What an ethic that preaches that work, whether or not it be for beneficial purposes, is deeply laudable, that work is the way to salvation, that work is not a means to an end, but the end itself? Oh, the glory of work without ceasing, work that has become the compulsive objective of the species. Have we not become like slack-mouthed beasts madly scurrying in an eternal circle, working, working, forevermore working.

In an earlier, perhaps healthier, time, work for its own sake was a foreign idea. As the philosopher and economist Max Weber demonstrated: in those societies that predate the Industrial Revolution, beginning as early as the tribe itself, man suffered no passion for work beyond the need to maintain his standard of living. The so-called workaholic is a casualty of the Industrial Age and is the piteous progeny of the religion of work. The cruelest punishment of all, one that would cause even the most heartless sadist to flinch, is to lay upon the life of man meaningless, empty work that uses him up like so much axle grease.

Today you can see him everywhere, the mad worker, scraping, scheming, toiling endlessly in a wild fury to build his moneymaking machine—the farm, the business, the great corporation—to which the worker as well has become enslaved. And the machine he has built, no matter how large and powerful, is but a cog in a yet larger money machine, which in turn is but part of a whole economy of machines that grind away, mostly under their own power. Before the Industrial Revolution, the machine was the tool of man. But today man, by his labor, has often become the fuel of the machine.

THE NEW SLAVE CHILDREN

The great industrial society could never have been set into motion but for the availability of an abundance of workers willing to be used up under the prevailing dogma of the religion of work—that work is good, that to slave all of one's life provides the road to salvation. And when the machine runs out of cheap-enough labor in America to provide fuel for itself, it reaches out to the overt slavery of the Third World, snatching up the labor of small girls who sew up our clothing and produce parts for our computers in dimly lit shacks with leaking roofs.

The labels inside do not say, "Made in Indonesia by children with blistered fingers and blinded eyes." The automobiles do not bear medallions that read, "Made in Mexico by workers who slave at the edge of hunger." And when I protest, the answer I get is, "Well, they'd be starving if they didn't get their fifty dollars a month. The little girls you worry about would be sold into prostitution if they didn't have that job." And so it is we forever hear the slave ghoul still making arguments to justify the evil of slavery.

John Calhoun made a similar argument a century and a half ago. "Slavery provides a positive good . . . the African race never existed so comfortably, so respectably, or in such a civilized condition." Today we strike the same bargain: we enjoy cheap clothes, the little girls do not starve as quickly and are not sold into prostitution as soon, and perhaps the workers in Mexico have a few more beans on the table.

The master cannot exist without slaves. The idea that God has, in his munificence, graced the planter, the businessman, the industrialist, the born rich with the divine right to enslave others has always been the central argument for slavery and is the origin of the work ethic that has been foisted upon the people.

THE IGNOMINY OF WORK

Work, as an abstract activity, has no merit when undertaken for itself. Prehistoric man did not work. He hunted, which was his pleasure. He gathered, which was his joy. Anthropologists insist that in his nascent state man was engaged but an hour or two a day in providing himself with food. And that was not work. It was man's play, his adventure, the fulfillment of his genetic purpose. Work was unknown to pre-historic man.

Smohalla, a Nez Percé Indian, saw work as evil:

> My young men shall never work. Men who work can-not dream, and wisdom comes to us in dreams.
>
> You ask me to plow the ground. Shall I take a knife and tear my mother's breast? Then when I die she will not take me to her bosom to rest.
>
> You ask me to dig for stone. Shall I dig under the skin for her bones? Then when I die I cannot enter her body to be born again.
>
> You ask me to cut grass and make hay and sell it and be rich like white men. But how dare I cut off my mother's hair?

Only a harsh master could force us to the relentless drudg-ery of meaningless, endless, numbing toil. The U.S. economist John Kenneth Galbraith observed, "Clearly the most unfortu-nate people are those who must do the same thing over and over again, every minute, or perhaps twenty to the minute. They deserve the shortest hours and the highest pay." The re-ligion of work is no less the cause of our anxiety than are other religions. It is against the religion of work to embrace the mo-ment, to feel, to experience one's relatedness to the earth and its occupants. According to the religion of work, it is insane to stop work and hug a tree. In light of the endless work that lies waiting, its foot tapping in impatience, it is irresponsible to stop and to wonder at the simple beauty of a forest fern.

The notion of work, and its puritanical elevation to the rank of the greatest virtues, is a religion that converts the diamonds of human creativity into the coal of the industrial machine. The religion of work has transformed human life and all of its potential, its great capacity for joy and fulfillment, into the inert fuel that is dumped into the furnaces of the New Master. Out of this religion is produced the gadgets and trinkets we purchase from the puddled sweat of our work, and out of this religion is produced the great war machinery that is destined one day to destroy the human race as the final vengeance of the insane machine against its insane inventors.

Yet I do not wish to confuse the idea of work on the one hand with that of slavery on the other. Work and slavery are not reciprocal concepts, although slaves work and work can become slavery. Merely because people work does not suggest that they are slaves. Free men work when their work is their joy. Free men work when they are also free not to work. They work but remain the masters of themselves.

WORK, THE VIRTUE THAT ENSLAVES

The elevation of the drudgery of work to a virtue is our dubious legacy from the Puritans. Luther and Calvin laid the way in the late Middle Ages. The renowned American psychoanalyst Erich Fromm thought that the Reformation's doctrine of predestination, which contends that God, at the time of our birth, had already determined who would and who would not be saved, created such an anxiety in man due to his not knowing his eternal fate that it was necessary for him to treat the pain of his anxiety with compulsive, meaningless activity.

Fromm likened the phenomenon of ceaseless work to a man awaiting the pronouncement of the doctor as to whether or not he is afflicted with a terminal disease. The man, waiting, waiting, paces the floor to alleviate his terrible anxiety.

But I believe the American worker does not engage in a fury of meaningless activity to ease the anxiety described by Fromm. I say that generally he works because he is enslaved.

In the new industrial state, the rich and the powerful, too, are compulsively at work, impelled by insatiable greed— greed born of man's terror of death, for no matter how hard and long he works, no matter how much money he accumulates, no matter how much power he wields, still he can never conquer death. Yet he cannot give up his life without attempting by ceaseless acquisition to achieve power over death. Here he stands, this puny man of the Protestants, bearing the burden of a free will that, at last, proves useless as a weapon against the grave.

The work ethic in America, flowering from the original doctrines of Luther and Calvin, fulfilled the requirements of the industrial state. Indeed, man might achieve salvation if he were honest, diligent, and responsible and worked hard according to the model set by Henry Ford, which is to say that man could enter the pearly gates if he in all ways qualified as a good, reliable, and efficient worker-slave. And he might feed his family as well. If he worked at lawful work, even at worthless work, even at work that might bring misery or death to many, even at work that might kill him, the worker, still, because of such work alone, could at last be judged as worthy.

One thinks of the workers at Los Alamos laboring away at the nuclear bomb that could, and perhaps one day will, destroy the world. One thinks of the workers in the tobacco fields and the cigarette factories. One thinks of the clever gurus laboring away on Madison Avenue, whose creative advertising will eventually hook three thousand kids every day on cigarettes. Such work is respected not because it produces good, but because it is work. Such workers are respected, not because they produce a useful product, but because the workers work.

Under the Puritan doctrines, even the sinner, if he worked hard enough, could finally earn the respect of his neighbors. Hard work was the only means by which the poor could, in the eyes of the community, rise above the degradation of their poverty. "He was an honest, hard-working man" were the words spoken over many a corpse.

Today we still embrace the empty ethic—if one works long enough and hard enough one will, if nothing else, receive the blessed kiss in heaven. Yet, on the last day, the difference between the worker and those who have snatched the fruits of his labor is that the former dies in a hard bed, the latter in a soft one.

I do not argue that people ought not work. But let us for once be practical about it. Likely one must work if one has not chosen his parents carefully and has not thrown off the troublesome habit of eating. Moreover, one must likely resort to work to acquire a mate and feed and educate the resulting aftermath. But aside from the plain necessity of work and its status as the most laudable evidence of a person's worth, what, I ask, is there about work that makes it intrisically right and blessed?

HERE LIES ELSIE

I say work is good mostly because out fathers and mothers have said it is good. It is good because our parents, dominated and enslaved, had to work and, as the Scriptures observe, the sins of the father are visited upon the child. It is good because our mothers worked and were enslaved by their work—the mother, the slave to the house, to the stove, to the bawling kids and the dirty diapers. How would we like to read on our tombstone, "Here lies Elsie. She was a slave to an eternity of diapers."? Well, she was. And she worked all of her life, and she was said to have had a good and fulfilling time of it because she was indentured to her kids and her kitchen and the pails—10,543 pails of dirty diapers by actual count.

A GOLD WATCH FOR HOMER

The old man slaved all of his life working as a bookkeeper at the railroad shops for ten, sometimes twelve hours a day. He was part of management. No overtime pay. And when he retired, they didn't even give him a gold watch. Gold watches are so much corporate propaganda. We all understand that. Maybe we wouldn't mind working all our lives for the company if, when we retired after thirty-some years, they'd at least give us a gold watch. But no. Like the old man, we get nothing but a swift boot in the hind end. Get out of here, you stinking old fogy. You are finished—used up. You can't even stand up straight—been hunkered over those books for so long.

One day after he retired the old man got cleaned up to go to the funeral of Mose, the master mechanics' foreman who worked with the old man those thirty-some years at the railroad. The old man looked in the mirror. He could see the clean gray hairs in his nose, and the little hair that had stayed the course on his head was washed and all frizzy. What the old man saw in the mirror everybody else had been seeing for a long time. It frightened him. He couldn't put words to it. Never was good at words.

He walked out the front door, and he stopped in the middle of the sidewalk and looked up at the sky as if he were waiting for the clouds to part and for a voice to say, "Homer, you done good. You were honest, and you never stole a friggin' nickel from the railroad, and you put the kid through junior college. You are an all right man, Homer. Plum all right. Hard worker."

But nobody and nothing said anything to the old man. Then he got into his Chevy Malibu and drove off to Mose's funeral. When he came home, he kicked the kid out of the house. "Been hangin' aroun' too damn long," he said. Kid almost twenty—finished junior college. Took a course in art. Could have gotten into advertising if he'd tried. Good money there, the old man argued. But the kid just wanted to paint a lot of silly paintings. Went through junior college, and he couldn't even paint a picture that looked like anything.

"You oughta go to work," the old man said. "Nothin' wrong with work, ya know. Make something of yerself. I was already workin' at the railroad when I was your age."

RIGHT WORK

Work in itself is not godly. Work in the abstract is not virtue. I do not disparage work as an honest means of survival. But work to feed the hungry face is not the first level of slavery. *The first level of slavery is the worship of work.*

Work that enables us to experience the deep pleasure of creativity is virtue. The potter throws his pot and experiences the ecstasy of his creativity. The farmer tills his fields, and feels the earth between his fingers and feels the joy of his work when the first potato sprouts poke though the soil. The carpenter steps back from the studs that will support the roof and feels the pleasure of his gift. The doctor administers to the sick with compassion, heals them, and feels the touch of God at his breast.

Work to free the self is virtue. Work to gain endless power

or endless wealth is not. Such work is but currying the deep misery of a frightened soul. Such work is but medicating a profound addiction to wealth that has grown out of bottomless insecurity. I say one must free one's self of the religion of work.

Thoreau insisted that man should not work for six days and rest on the seventh. Instead, he argued, man should work one day and leave six free for the "sublime revelations of nature." In the end, if the worker has served the work rather than having the work serve him, he is enslaved.

THE BETTER-FITTED ZOO

In America, freedom and work are often incompatible bed partners. We are free to work, all right, and we are also free to go hungry and become homeless. But, as we have seen, many want neither freedom nor work. They want to frolic around in a better-fitted zoo. They want to loll about in an easy bed and sell themselves for a higher price so they can buy more beads and more trinkets. They want those long warm winter vacations and bigger TVs and fancy basketball shoes. They want to *feel* free by driving a certain sports car. They want to swagger and *look* free by wearing certain "out-there" clothing, and to come off as free by smoking a certain brand of cigarette. They are willing to indenture themselves in order to buy the *symbols* of freedom sold by the ad-makers on Madison Avenue, but they do wish to experience freedom.

They want to bellow on talk shows with great asperity about their First Amendment rights, and their civil rights, their right to remain silent and their right to die and their right to life. They want the right to harass without being harassed, but they do not want to experience freedom. No. All this talk about freedom is too often just self-serving palaver exhaled in six-second sound bites to entertain us.

THE BREAD-SNATCHERS

I know many a rich man who says he accumulates wealth to "keep score," whatever that means. But how can the hoarding of money "to keep score" be acceptable human conduct? Consider a dollar as a loaf of bread. Ten dollars equals ten loaves of bread. What do a million, a billion loaves of bread look like?

Do you see the children, the hungry children? What of the billionaire whose excuse for his billions is his need to "keep score." What is this insane game? Having acquired the first billion loaves, must he seek another billion? And, of course, he must protect his bread from being stolen. He must protect it even from the hungry children.

Can you see the bread piled up high, the billion loaves towering to the sky, covering whole blocks of a city, a high fence around the city of bread to protect it? Can you see the children, their faces pushed up against the fence, their protruding stomachs, their wide eyes eyeing but a part of a loaf? Where is the virtue in this game? Is this not an evil game, a mad game played by madmen? If one of these bread-snatchers should give away a few loaves of bread, we call him a philanthropist, and we admire him. If he speaks, we listen with great respect. I am not arguing for a Marxist solution. I am simply freeing our minds of the myth that there is virtue in the mindless, endless accumulation of wealth.

THE FOURTH STEP TO FREEDOM:
PLAYING OUR LIVES AWAY

When young people ask me what they should do, I say, "Play. Play all of your life away." I have played away much of mine doing what many would consider work. No one ever asks me, "What are you playing at?" They assume I must be working, sitting here writing these words, standing there in the courtroom speaking those words. I could not be without my play. It does not burden. It frees. It does not exhaust me with deadly drudgery. It sends me into the depths for an archeological dig of the self, where all our unknown treasures abound.

If one's play results in money, that is an acceptable side effect, like the strengthening of the heart that comes from a joyous walk up a mountain. Play. *I say, play your life away.* Play until you are worn-out, for play is the fulfillment of your life. Play as bees play, flitting from flower to flower gathering the honey, and as bears play, climbing the bee tree for the honey. Play exalts the gifts of God to man—his talent, his creative energy, his uniqueness—fulfilling him by what brings him joy, which is his play.

If there be God, certainly God played when he made the universe. You can see the pleasure. God must have been fiddling around in the firmament, creating order and disorder, amusing himself in his infinite creations, lolling about in eternity. If man, then, is created in the image of God, ought he not play as well?

In a broader sense, as religion serves the aristocracy of money, as it bows to the god of business, as it recites the dogma of free enterprise on the one hand or of socialism on the other, we trudge into a strange and frightening world— a world where religion, not people, is paramount. In that unearthly world the Holy Ghost is not a loving God, but an enslaving force; not a freeing spirit, but a master that enslaves us through myth and fear and, at last, through madness.

The Magical Power of Aloneness

*I went to the woods because I wished to live delib-
erately, to front only the essential facts of life, and
see if I could not learn what it had to teach, and not,
when I came to die, discover that I had not lived.*

—HENRY DAVID THOREAU
from *Walden,* 1854

THE MYSTICAL POWER OF ALONENESS

Let me take you to a forest in the high mountain country of
Wyoming. The spruce and lodge pole pines rise as tall as
grasses to the ant. No sound except the wind through the
needles. No sound except the chipping of an irreverent squirrel. And then no sound at all.

I have stood there as a frightened child, the snow falling,
each horizon looking the same, the same towering trees in
every direction blotting the way, the forest brimming with
ghosts, with the staring dead, and perhaps, I thought, with
grizzlies too.

I have stood there too frightened to breathe. One would
not dare cry out in fear. One would dare not break the hush
with the sound of one's voice, tiny and high as a peeping
chick smashing into the silence, for the universe would surely

come hurling down in an avalanche of fury and scoop one up into the horrible void.

I have stood there alone in the forest waiting for my father to return from the hunt to fetch me, like a doe returning for her deposited fawn. I have strained my eyes to see his dark form appear from the shadows, his legs, long and sure, the toes turned slightly in like those of an Indian. Where is he? I peer into the trees ahead, but the way is dark, and the snow falls on the lids and leaves large drops on the lashes. What has happened to my father? He is the only God I know, for he is the only God I can see. What if God, who is up in the sky, who is everywhere watching—what if he is angry at me? The terror of it. To be alone in the forest where even the sound of one's breath must be eased from the nostrils, for even the breath can awaken the devil.

To be alone on the earth is the abysmal terror. Fish swim in schools. Birds fly in flocks. The buffalo wander in herds. And man has his tribe. Alone in the forest, the boy is free, but the aloneness is unbearable, and the freedom it provides is fear.

Now I see the movement through the shadows. I stare, my eyes bulging like the eyes of a fawn in panic. The movement is in my direction. I cannot make out its form in the shadows. Then I see my father moving easily through the trees. He walks as silently as any forest creature. Now he sees me, and he smiles. The face, the face of God, the snow gathering on his shoulders, the steam coming from his lungs. He has come for me, and all is right in the world once more, and I will never, no never, be alone again.

As he walks up to where I stand, it is as if he had never left, as if I had never been alone. His presence is the infinite magic of God. He has changed my world in an instant. The hunting was good. You can see it on his hands—the blood, the brown elk hair stuck to them, and the small pack on his back that bulges with the elk's heart and liver.

What is it in the human soul that so fears aloneness? We are born in the presence of our mothers, but only we, alone, experience our birth. We may be in the presence of others at death, but only we, alone, will experience our death. It is the fear of death that terrorizes—the fear of the unknown. To be alone is equated with death. Banishment from the tribe is death. Alone, one is vulnerable to the attack of one's enemies. Alone, one may be killed and eaten like a deer separated from the herd and run down by wolves. Aloneness warns of the impending end.

Yet the fear of death is irrational. Socrates thought death quite fine. Death would deliver him to his friends or drop him gently into a dreamless sleep. To him, either was acceptable. And John Dryden wrote:

> *Death is nothing; but we fear*
> *To be we know not what,*
> *We know not where.*

The irrational fear of death has, of course, a biological purpose. If the species is not blessed with the fear of death, it cannot escape danger. It cannot survive. We hurl the young and foolish into battle because the young have never seen the face of death and are not so afraid. Old men never fight. Old men are old because they have heard the trumpeter and know his song.

Alone.

Without aloneness, without taking the fear of it into the self, without knowing it, what is the use? Birth and death happen there. And life as well happens there. The power of the self happens there. The rest is distraction. The rest is escape for those who have grown afraid of themselves.

I have never known a daffodil that failed to bloom because it stood alone. I have never known a chickadee who failed to fly because it struggled alone in learning the use of its wings. I have never known a man who grew unless he experienced alone time to discover himself.

Alone. Then is when it happens. In silence, alone. The radio off. How could the radio in the car be off? I have seen people panic at such silence, grab for the knob, like a drowning person for the life buoy. When the voice on the radio is off, they are like ducklings who, when the mallard mother has ceased her soft quacking, swim in tight little circles in a great pool of terror. Today telephones are installed in hotels and in many modern homes so that the person seated on the bathroom throne can reach out to the phone and converse with someone, probably anyone, even while he experiences the most common (and blessed) act of being alone. Cell phones now insure us that we need not be alone while we drive, while we eat, while we walk down the street. Our television sets protect us from being alone, even for a few moments in the morning while we drink our first cup of coffee and at night before we crawl into bed. Thoreau wrote in *Walden,* "I have a great deal of company in my house; especially in the morning, when nobody calls."

OUT OF ALONENESS — THE POWER OF THE SELF

People who do not experience aloneness have breathed only the stale air of others. But in aloneness I say it happens. I write alone—my gift to myself and to you. I dream alone. I feel, and the feelings are mine, out of my aloneness, out of my belly, out of the place beneath my heart, out of the hidden place where "the he who is me" exists, alone. To find one's self, to clearly hear one's self, to feel the crisp, pure texture of one's self, to be one's best student and the devoted teacher of the self—there is where the bloom of the person bursts free.

We wish to be swallowed up. "Swallow me up," we cry to the mob called the system. "Take me." It is better to be taken than to be alone. It is better to be a slave in the presence of slaves than to be free in the presence of only the self—the frightening, lonely, terrorized self. Henry David Thoreau was alone when he wrote, "I have never found the companion that was so companionable as solitude."

Out of aloneness rises the power of the self. It will face the man within, affirm him, and learn to respect, yes, even to love him. Out of aloneness is built the shelter of the self. It is the most secure of all places on earth. No citadel offers such protection, no fortress such safety. Once one has found the shelter of the self, the need for the authority of another, for the authority of the guru, for the authority of the government, for the authority of the church, for religion's authority, for God's, vanishes.

THE AUTHORITY OF THE SELF

Already God has given his authority over man to man himself. It is called free will. God does not want it back, for authority is worthless to God. Why should He covet authority? What can God, the ultimate authority, do with any more authority? And what loving God wishes to be worshipped? Do we not understand that he who requires worship is insecure in himself? Do we believe that God is insecure? It is we who need the worshipping, not God who requires the worshipping. It is we, the frightened, the alone, who seek the object of worship, and we call him or her God, and fall on our knees and pray out of our dismal fear of aloneness.

If, indeed, we are to achieve the kingdom of God, we must first achieve the kingdom of the self. Truth does not set us free. *The self sets us free.* And should we come face-to-face with the self, we shall come face-to-face with the final authority—the final authority not for another, not for the neighbor, nor for the child, but for the self. And that is enough. And that is godly.

ALONENESS, THE WAY TO FREEDOM

When I speak of aloneness, I do not mean loneliness. Alone or not, one may, indeed, long for friends and a mate. On the other hand, one may possess friends and a mate and still experience loneliness. When I speak of aloneness, I am speaking of the experience, lonely or not, of being alone.

Yet when I walk though the woods alone, I am not alone. I have simply chosen my companion. I encounter my relationship to the world around me. My aloneness explodes into the exquisite, moving, intense company of the self. I feel the mystery—yes, the spiritual. I sense an attachment to the world that I rarely experience in the company of others. Alone, I am not alone. Some call the experience God.

I have often enjoyed the company of others as we have walked together in the woods. And while the experience of togetherness may be enhanced by the surrounding serenity and beauty of the forest, the experience is utterly different from walking through the same woods alone. Walking with a companion in nature, as pleasurable as it may be, is like walking into a theater where a great orchestra is performing. Having entered the theater, we now walk down the aisle speaking at the top of our voices, and, without concern, walk right on through the orchestra itself, still talking.

As a part of my teaching of young trial lawyers at my ranch, I send them out to be alone in nature. I send them out in the dark before the sun is up and instruct them to find a place where they can see and hear no other living person. They are to find a place that they can call their place—a place on a rock, by a tree, along the river, out on the prairie, or at the top of a mountain—any place that they can claim as their own place away from all others. Here they are to sit quietly alone awaiting the sunrise.

For many of these students, this is the first time they have intentionally set out to experience themselves alone. This is the first opportunity most have had to ask themselves the simple questions "Who am I, and where am I going?" When, after several hours, they return to share their experience with their fellows, invariably they have been struck with deep and powerful emotions. Many weep, not out of pain, but out of the profound joy of having experienced the self for the first time. Some have written poetry. Some have gathered stones, or a feather or a small piece of wood that will stand as a remembrance of their experience. Almost without exception they are shocked and delighted at having met the person within, whom they have held imprisoned from themselves all of their lives.

A STORY

I recently received a letter from a friend:

Let me tell you a story—a little Christmas story: It's Saturday evening. I'm sitting restlessly in my room. I tap my head against the wall. Oh, I'm so lonely. I think: My friends are already on their way to a party—I'm sure of that. But I don't want to party tonight. Yet this damned loneliness . . . maybe I should have gone with them. Oh, I wish somebody would call me. But only the darkness is here, an unpleasant, empty silence, a vacuum in my restless body.

I put on a CD to fill the empty silence with techno. I try to kill my loneliness with noise and pumping beats. Boom. Boom. Boom. But I'm only getting more restless. It is as if a band of small teasing pixies were constantly pushing me and yelling nasty things into my ears. I can't find peace. . . .

I stop the techno. I simply choose to listen to the silence—the silence that before I was so afraid of. I choose to feel the restlessness and the loneliness. After a little while the pixies stop their teasing and look at me very surprised. I look back—calmly, just waiting. Then they yawn, blink their eyes, and go to bed in the creases of my clothes.

I have returned to my center. Gradually I have come beneath the restlessness, and down there I find peace. A lovely, soft warmth fills my body, and my brain is gearing down. I'm able to enjoy the new silence that consists of peace instead of the unpleasant, empty silence from before.

Thus it became a wonderful evening in front of the fireplace. . . . I'm so happy I didn't go to that party to fill out the emptiness with techno, alcohol, a lot of teasing pixies, and the hangover. Instead I have filled the emptiness with peace, with Christmas and the feeling of being alive.

The Magical Power of Aloneness

I do not mean that one must live alone. I do not mean that one must not enjoy a mate or friends, that one must not communicate with others, that one cannot learn from others, that one cannot become a member of a tribe, a club, a community, or a nation. I say only that *freedom is the gift of the self,* and this gift of all gifts is not given in the presence of the car radio, or the television, or the jabber of friends. It is not given in the madness of a sporting event, or the insanity of the workplace. It is not given in the conjugal bed. It is not the gift of the pope or of a political party. Freedom is the gift of the self, to the self, and it is given and received best when the self is alone.

Withholding Permission to Lose

*However sugarcoated and ambiguous, every form
of authoritarianism must start with a belief in some
group's greater right to power . . .*

— GLORIA STEINEM

from *Ms.*, New York, October/November 1980

RECOGNIZING THE ENEMY

How often I have encountered the enemy. The enemy comes
in many forms:

The enemy is our sense of duty to those to whom we owe
no duty.

The enemy is our fear when it causes us to quake like a
rabbit before a drooling lion, when, instead, we should embrace our fear as the source of our strength.

The enemy is the bastard voice from within that has been
implanted by society, by religion, by parents and teachers
who assert we are helpless and powerless.

The enemy is the venemous voice that whispers over and
over that we are impotent and weak and not worth a whit in
a windstorm.

The enemy is everywhere, encountered daily, experienced
at work, in a system that shows us no respect, that reduces
us to lifeless plodding automatons.

The enemy is the fish in the school of millions of fish that does not realize his smallness is as mighty as the greatness of the great whale, that no one harpoons a minnow and sells its blubber.

The enemy most often encountered today is *our vision of ourselves*—as only another digit on a balance sheet. The enemy is our vision of ourselves—as an insignificant and anonymous occupant of the streets, where we merge like blades of grass with millions to make up the lawn, which the master in turn mows as he pleases, and upon which the master frolics.

The enemy says we have already been subdued. We are already owned by the system. We are already hopelessly enslaved.

The enemy says we were born into the ghetto of servitude, when, instead, we were born in a palace of freedom.

The enemy lies to us. The enemy says that to be free we must become rich and powerful. And the lies are deep and enslaving. The lies destroy our children, squash their free hearts, box in the pain of their traps and box out the joy of their growth. The lies against our children tell our children they are not perfect. The lies tell our children they are not beautiful and worthy, that they must submit to fear—fear of their puny selves, fear of the power of others, fear of a God who watches them like the eternal voyeur in the sky, fear of free thought, fear of the new, fear of their own blessed individuality and creativity. Such lies to our children are the gifts of slavery.

A cab driver was talking to me the other day on my way to the courthouse. "Me, I ain't nothin'. Me, I'm just a cabby. Nobody gives a shit about me. The only difference between me an' ever'body else is that me, well, nobody sees me. But if I'd been the limo driver for O. J. Simpson, I woulda been seen. I woulda been somebody then." He laughed an unlaughing laugh.

To be seen! To be somebody! The cabby had, of course, given the power to *them,* whoever they are. If they chose to look at him, he could thereby become somebody, or they could condemn him to eternal nothingness by refusing to see him at all. In the cabby's view, one cannot be special without *them* saying so. I think of the flower in the deepest forest. Is it not equally beautiful whether seen by me or not?

We are told that unless we are recognized by *them,* we are nothing. Unless we are approved by the boss, by our spouse, by somebody, anybody, we are worthless. We are told that unless the priest or the clergyman blesses us, we cannot achieve salvation. Unless we submit to the religion of our parents, we will be condemned to eternal damnation. Unless we bow to the religion of free enterprise, we will be viewed as un-American. Unless we respect those who are disrespectful of us, we will be banished.

WINNING: WITHHOLDING PERMISSION
TO BE DEFEATED

The enemy has extracted from us our *permission* to be defeated, subdued, manipulated, used, and used up. There was a time in my life when, young and inexperienced, but full of fight and brimming with divine ignorance, I was losing civil cases for deserving clients—for the waitress whose small boy was injured and who, because I lost her case, could not provide medical help for her son; for the farmer who had been cheated out of his crop by a scam artist, and who was in danger of losing his farm because I couldn't get justice for him. The losses were painful—almost too painful to endure. I felt as if a sword had been thrust through me and I was bleeding to death. I saw deserving clients walk out of the courtroom with their heads down and their faces empty of hope. I had no excuse. I had prepared. I had done my best. But I had lost nevertheless.

"Why do I need this pain?" I asked.

"You need the pain because you have lost cases that you should not have lost," the voice within spoke back. "Do you see that crippled boy who will now go through life without proper medical attention and who was entitled to justice? You suffer the pain because you should suffer the pain. You deserve it," the voice said.

"Why did I lose?" I asked.

There was no response from the talkative self. Silence.

"Why did I lose?" I demanded again. Still there was silence for many days. At last I thought I had lost because I was unskilled, because I was inexperienced. I was weak and worthless was the charge. I lost because I had no talent. I lost because I was ignorant, perhaps stupid. How could the likes of me ever win?

I had never graduated from a big university. I knew no powerful people. There were, perhaps, more people in a square block of New York City or Chicago on a given day than in the whole state of Wyoming. Besides that, I didn't understand all the cartoons in the *New Yorker*. Still don't. How could a country lawyer win against the fancy city lawyers with the pretty suits and the pretty language and the slick minds and the heavy intelligence that came slamming against me like indomitable waves?

I was nothing. I needed power. I prayed.

But the prayer gave away the power I had already been given. The prayer needed to be directed to the self, where all of the power I sought was already vested. An old woman once said to me, "You already have what you seek."

As always, in the darkness of the early morning, in that state when the conscious and the unconscious wrestle for power, the voice came to me. Without providing answers, it asked questions.

"Why," the voice asked, "do you give your adversaries *permission* to beat you? Do you need to be defeated? Is the pain of defeat necessary in your life? You try. But trying is not winning. Trying is only what you do after you have given *permission to be defeated*."

Suddenly I saw it! What is true is always simple. *They could not have defeated me without my permission.*

We give permission for them to defeat us when we adopt as our appraisal of ourselves that view imposed upon us by *them*. We give permission to be stepped upon when we see ourselves as ants, as, indeed, we are seen by *them*, by those to whom we have given our power.

I am not speaking of an obnoxious arrogance. I am speaking of our failure to make an accurate appraisal of our power. I do not demand that they change their view of me. *I only demand that I change my view of myself.* How can *they* defeat me if I do not give them permission to defeat me?

They can own my property, they can imprison me in their walls, they can deprive me of justice, they can speak better and more eloquently than I. They can wield their power over me from high places—from the bench, from the pulpit, from city hall. But without my permission they cannot defeat me. They can withhold their favorable judgment, they can withhold what I seek, but, at last, they cannot defeat *me*.

THE STATURE OF POWER

It is a stature, a position, an image of oneself that without consciousness is communicated to our adversaries. My brother, Tom, speaks of it. He has lived major portions of his adult life in the dangerous parts of the city and has never been mugged. Never attacked. It is an aura, not put on, but a genuine sense of the self that is communicated in the walk, the language of the face, in the way of the person. It is not a fierce mask. It is a powerful soul, empowered by the self that refuses to give permission to be defeated, and the presence of which is strangely apparent.

You see it in animals. A certain dog's dominance is established, and he is not always the larger or stronger. Rarely do two dogs fight to establish the hierarchy. More often they sidle up to one another, take each other in, the back hair up, the stiff, hostile tail wagging, the fighting teeth exposed. Then one walks away, and at that moment both know which of them holds the power, which has refused to give permission to be defeated. In the wolf pack, the alpha wolf prevails. In the boxing ring, the physically stronger man does not always win. The victor is usually he who has refused to give permission to be defeated.

PERMISSION TO BE ENSLAVED

The essential elements of slavery can be identified in the makeup of nearly every culture from the beginning of civilization. When civilization was developing, the slave and the master were defined and became the opposing forces that supported the culture. Nothing has changed. Only the face of the culture has changed. Slavery, as we have seen, takes whatever form, whatever disguise, dons whatever mask as may be necessary for one class to wield its power over another. And as long as there are people who give their permission to be defeated, to be denigrated and oppressed, to be used and used up, there will be those who will oblige them.

We give permission for *them* to enslave us when we take their judgments of us as our own:

When the teacher tells the child that her drawing does not look like a tree,

When the professor tells the student he has no talent,

When the psychologist tells the person he is abnormal,

When the doctor tells the patient she is neurotic,

When the lawyer tells the client his case is worthless,

When human beings are judged by the color of their skin, the place they live, the language they employ, the dress they wear, the car they drive,

When the banker tells a young person she cannot prevail in business,

When the entrepreneur discourages a new idea,

When we are told that our most passionate goals are impossible, or our most heartfelt longings, stupid,

When we are adjudged to be slow, or dull, or unimaginative,

When we are compared unfavorably to others—to a brother, to a friend, to some other who is pushed up in our faces—

These are the judgments that have been foisted upon us daily. When we accept them as judgments of ourselves, we in turn grant others permission to enslave us.

GRANTING PERMISSION TO BE JUDGED

By what right do others judge us? By what authority? *They judge us by the authority we have given them to judge us.* We cannot prevent them from making their judgments, but their judgments are empty and impotent unless *we* accept their judgments as legitimate for us.

We even permit others whom we do not know, and whom we do not care to know, to judge us. I am often amused at our concern for our appearance. We dress to the teeth to go to a formal dinner party, lending extreme care to our appearance for the benefit of a public that does not know us and, unless we have dressed in some greatly inappropriate way, will give no more thought to us than we give to them as we stroll to our own tables. At the same time we may wear the sloppiest clothes and maintain the most uncomely appearance among the people closest to us, who will surely see us and make note of our person. I am not against spiffing up a bit from time to time. I am commenting only on how we deliver to strangers the power to judge us. The power is in our minds, and by the wheelbarrow of our minds, we deliver the power to them. Eleanor Roosevelt once said, "No one can make you feel inferior without your consent."

RESPECTING THE RESPECTABLE

The noble crown of respect should be affixed to the head of every person who has achieved the *status of personhood.* By those who have achieved *personhood* I mean those who have not only empowered themselves, and thereby respect themselves as their final authority, but who hold a deep and enduring respect for *every person,* no matter how humble.

But should the slave therefore respect the master? Should we respect the employer who cares more about profit than about the welfare of his workers? Should we respect the corporate overseers who are incapable of respecting their most menial workers, who see them as mere mechanisms to accomplish the assigned tasks of production? Should we respect the money monger whose primary passion is his insatiable greed?

Should we respect the hog merely because it is fat?

How do we respect a judge who is committed not to justice but to the power interests that have enthroned him? How do we respect the law when it is more committed to the protection of property than to the protection of the well-being of the people?

As a young lawyer I was instructed by old heads of the bar that we should "respect the robe" no matter what judge wore it. When the old heads demanded that I respect the robe, I was really being asked to respect their cronies, the men they put on the bench with their money and their influence. When they asked me to endow the robe with respect, without regard to the rogue who wore it, they asked me to respect *their* power over my client's right to justice. When I give respect to the robe, I lose the right to rise up against the injustice imposed by a judge who wears it. Similarly we are admonished to respect our elders. How do we respect certain elders who, given the power, would, at the drop of a penny, enslave us? Is it not true that fools, too, grow old, and as old men are merely old fools?

RESPECTING THOSE CLOSEST TO ANGELS

I have seen many a parent, too many—and as a young man I found myself among them—who did not fully understand the respect the child deserves from the parent. "Children are to be seen, not heard" was the old cruel, enslaving saw. Teach the child to respect what is not respectable and you teach the child the first tenet of slavery—submission to unjust authority. Children are persons. They are small persons whose perfect souls have not yet been ground through the meat grinder of slavery.

Children, as persons, are entitled to the greatest respect. Children are given to us as free flying souls, after which we clip their wings in the same way we domesticate the wild mallard. Children should become our role models for they are coated with the spirit from which they came—out of the ether, clean, innocent, brimming with the delight of life, aware of the beauty of the simplest thing—a snail, a bud, a shadow in the garden. Children are closest to the angels.

I say that we must respect children as we respect sages, as we respect the venerable of history. Give me the wisdom of a child rather than the erudite colloquies of Samuel Johnson. I say that we should look upon the child as our teacher, that we should learn to free the soul as the child's soul is free. Like the child, must we not learn to cry out at the joy of small discoveries, to express our anger and our fear, our love and our loneliness? How delightful to be delighted as the child is delighted. Like the child, must we not learn to be with the self as the happy child is happy with the self, to ask as the child asks, to know that not to know is all right, to learn that ignorance is the beginning of all knowledge?

No child takes anything on faith except the love of his parent and the goodness of the species. I say that of all the occupants of the earth—including the great persons of science, the artists, the caring healers, the true statesmen, the saints, and all others who have achieved the *status of persons*—the child is entitled to the greatest respect, for the child has lately been closest to God.

RESPECT, YES—SUBMISSION, NEVER!

Respect offered out of fear is not respect, but submission. Submission to God or man or to the religious madhouses of every description constructed by man transports one into the endless tunnel of slavery. Respect for the bully, whatever form he may take, is our entry into the tunnel.

I remember my father telling me when I was a child that I should not be afraid of the bully. But I *was* afraid of the bully, and therefore I thought myself a coward. My father said, "When the bigger kid knocks you down, get up. And when he knocks you down again, get up again. And get up every time he knocks you down. After a while it will be he, not you, who is afraid. He will learn you cannot be beaten. You can be knocked down, but you cannot be beaten." But I was still afraid.

My father was speaking to me about *permission*. One cannot respect the bully whom we encounter daily in numerous forms, nor give the bully permission to defeat us. Permission is given when we respect overt power merely because it is power. Overt power ought not be respected simply because it appears powerful. We may decide to protect ourselves from it. We may, being sensible, not confront it. But we do not respect it. Do we respect the brutal police because of their power? Do we respect the goose-steppers because of their power? Fear and respect are not the same.

I feared the bully, but I did not respect him. And had I been brave, which I was not, he would not have beaten me. Only by killing me with an ax could he have beaten me, and then he would not have beaten me. He would only have killed me. Such is the indomitable spirit that lies at the bedrock of every person. Yet layer on layer of the stultifying judgments of others prevents us from accessing the spirit—the spirit of the invincible. It is such spirit that permits the meek to prevail over the tyrant, whose piteous weapon is but rank power.

I once received a letter from a seventy-five-year-old woman in which she told me that she had been wrongfully dealt with by a multinational corporation over an increase in her rent. No one in the company would talk to her—not the CEO, not the manager, not the company lawyer—no one. After two-and-a-half years of being stonewalled, she decided to take the matter into her own hands. She went to the county, bought a peddler's permit to sell pencils, and began selling them in front of the company office. She said that no one could imagine the flurry of activity this caused. She said that old friends became distant and critical. How could she do such a thing? She was a nuisance. Some called her a smart-ass. The company lawyer tried to intimidate her, but instead of being intimidated, she threatened to walk out of the meeting that the company had finally arranged in order to settle this embarrassing matter. Finally the company gave in. The two hundred dollars a month she won wasn't much, she said. But, in the end, it was everything.

"IT TAKES TWO TO TANGO"

"It takes two to tango," they say. It also takes two to create slavery—a master and a slave. Each is utterly dependent on the other. In the same way, one cannot be dominated or manipulated without one's permission.

We can be fired by the boss, but we have not been fired from the self.

We can be thrown out of the club, but we have not been thrown out of the self.

We can be disdained, mocked, hated, rejected, banished,

excommunicated, but this does not mean we have been defeated. Defeat takes two. It takes a conqueror and a vanquished who agrees to surrender.

I do not speak of intractable rebelliousness as a way of life. Self-destruction is not liberty. What I denounce is our delivering to anyone or any group permission to conquer our soul, to extract from us our permission to be defeated. Defeat comes only when we have given permission to be conquered, when we feel defeat in the deepest lining of the belly, when we acknowledge it and submit to it in the most tender marrow of the self.

BLESSED FEAR

Sometimes I have looked into the face of a client and seen fear. Sometimes I have looked into my own face and seen it. Fear is the protector of life. It is the genetic implant of survival. The great buck with the majestic stance and the widespread horns is the first to bolt at the snap of a twig, for he knows danger, fears it, and has survived to become the lord of the forest. Despite his fear, he is the king. The small buck who knows no fear, who encounters danger but does not recognize it, stands before the hunter, his eyes blinking, and soon his liver is sizzling in the hunter's frying pan.

Fear was the friend of the old buck. In the same way fear is the friend of man. Although the big buck in the forest responded to fear, he did not give it permission to defeat him. He avoided the hunter's bullet, but he did not give up the majesty of the self. He was majestic in retreat, his great antlers shining in the sun, his neck expanded, his head thrown back. He was free to run, to hide, and to survive.

I say, embrace fear as a friend. It is nature's gift to us. It is the best weapon for freedom. When we acknowledge its presence, we do not give anyone permission to enslave us. Instead, it permits us to escape into the forest if we must. But it does not prevent the boy from rising off the ground one more time to defeat the bully. Fear is presented to us as a signal of danger. It permits us to escape or, because of it, to fight with a magically expanded power.

When once I learned that simple lesson, I could no longer be defeated in the courtroom. I have faced opposing counsel armed with endless expense accounts and whole armies of backup lawyers who finally gave up. I have had lawyers from the mammoth firms fold with heart attacks, or refuse to come out for the final argument. It is not because I am brighter, more powerful, better schooled, or even better prepared. It is not because I am braver than they. It is because they had waited, waited, and finally waited in panic, for me to grant permission to be defeated. When permission did not come, they were left alone with weapons that proved useless.

That a person is indomitable in his advocacy instills its message in the enemy. Once more the small boy rises up from the dirt. Once more the weak and the powerless withhold their permission to be defeated and become the ultimate power in the courtroom, in the boardroom, in the workplace, in every place. And those who contest it, feel the power. It is not a power spoken in a loud voice. It is not a power coated in anger. It is not an intransigent power that ignores the rights and feelings of others. It is a power so deeply rooted in the person that it becomes the person. The judge feels it. The jury feels it. Every adversary feels it. The power of the indomitable when aligned with justice cannot be defeated, for defeat, at last, requires permission of the vanquished.

THE SIXTH STEP TO FREEDOM: WITHHOLDING
PERMISSION TO BE DEFEATED —
REMEMBERING BOB ROSE

I think of my dear friend Robert R. Rose. He was past eighty years of age when he died. He was blind. He could not breathe without the oxygen tubes in his nostrils. His heart was too weak to endure the bypass surgery he required. He could not walk across the room without panting. He called me shortly before he died wanting to talk about the opening statement he was about to make to a jury. He was excited. His voice sounded like the voice of a young warrior. His case was just. His excitement was about his learning, about his ever-expanding self. He was so consumed with life, he had no time for dying.

The man could not be defeated. Not then. Not ever. He had given his life to the cause of justice, having served many years as the chief justice of the Wyoming Supreme Court and before and since as a trial lawyer. He was a teacher and mentor. But one part of the self he would not give—and that was permission to be defeated.

I was with him when he died. He was surrounded by his wife, his secretary of many years, his son and daughter, another close friend, and me. His eyes had failed. He could not see us. But he could hear that we were with him. The breathing tube was down his throat, so he could not speak. But that did not prevent his lips from forming words as he stared into the space I occupied.

"I love you," the lips said, and he reached up to feel where I was, and he found my face, and he felt it, and stroked my hair. And after that, we were with him when he made his decision. His lungs were filling from a failed heart. The heart was too weak for an operation, the lungs were gone, the heart was going, but not the spirit. Not the power of the self, even at death.

I remember how we held on to him, as if holding on to him would allow him to stay one more hour. His wife and children were at his head, his wife holding a hand, his daughter with her head at the side of his old racked ribs, and his son holding his other hand. We held on to his bare feet, one each, his secretary and I. And then, still retaining his power over life, he gave the sign—the cutting motion of the hand across the space in front of him. It was time. His time. His decision. Not ours. Not the doctors'.

Then the nurse came, and she removed the tube from his throat, which had provided life's oxygen to the caked old lungs, and he motioned that his dentures should be put back in. No one wants to go without one's dentures. He was calm, as if he were waiting for the waiter to bring him his soup. For him it was not a matter of bravery, but his approach to his birth.

We were with him. His wife spoke softly to him, as did his children, but by now he was alone. We were the rocks and the music in his garden, and he walked through the place, quietly. We watched the monitor that told us of his oxygen intake and his blood pressure and the beat of his heart. They began to slow, of course. It took an hour, perhaps a little more. Then he left us, walking on into the firmament, while we still held on, not wishing to go with him, but glad for him, and in deep awe of the miracle of death.

Finally the machine told us it was over. And I knew he had gone. The face was relaxed; the muscles of the mouth that had fought so many word wars, that had argued so long for justice, that had delivered so many sounds of love, were soft and easy. The monitor said the blood was clinically void of oxygen, the blood pressure, level.

"He's gone," the nurse confirmed even though his old heart continued to quiver, refusing even then to stop. Still, having watched him go, I was surprised at his having left, like someone who awakens to find his wife has risen silently from the bed while he slumbered. Then a great cloud of peace descended into the room, and the peace soaked up the sadness.

We stood together beside him, still holding on, staring at the monitor, taking one last look at the old shell that was no longer relevant to the man. In nearly forty years, although we were often apart, I had never felt his absence. Suddenly I felt lessened, as if something important had been stripped from me. Once more I was the child alone in the forest. But even as we left the room, his old heart did not give permission. As we left, I saw its faint movements on the screen. I doubt it will ever stop.

Rejecting the Slavery of Security

Probably the only place where a man can feel really secure is in a maximum security prison, except for the imminent threat of release.

—GERMAINE GREER
from *The Female Eunuch*, 1970

THE INSECURITY OF SLAVERY

Slavery provides a special kind of security—security from making one's own decisions, security from thinking for one's self, security from being responsible for one's acts, and security from experiencing one's life. A strange security persists—the security *against being free.*

Only the dead are utterly secure.

The struggle between freedom and security is eternal. The American colonists, by wresting their liberty from the king, gave up the security of his protection, of his armies and his powerful navy. They gave up the security of his laws, and of his exchequer. Yet there is no security under the yoke. The chicken in the chicken house is not secure. Saved from the coyote, the chicken will be eaten by the farmer.

The exchange of work for security is a false bargain. We have always known it. If the worker is not first thrown out as excess, he is excessively used and thus used up.

The master can never offer security. How can we be secure and become property? How can we be secure when we can be discarded like the potato peeling after the potato has been eaten? What security abounds when the master's intelligence is substituted for our own, when our creativity is stunted and ignored? What security is there when we grow old in the traces?

THE DEVIL'S BARGAIN

To give up freedom for security is the devil's bargain. Having made the bargain, one enjoys neither freedom nor security. Every slave is a machine. The master cares for his machinery until it is worn out or outmoded, or until, on a passing whim, the master obtains different machinery. In 1833 a large South Carolina planter spoke of the machinery of his plantation:

> A plantation might be considered as a piece of machinery. To operate successfully, all of its parts [the slaves] should be uniform and exact, and the impelling force regular and steady; and the master, if he pretended at all to attend to his business, should be their impelling force.

Today the corporate manager seeks uniformity with the same great passion—an army of workers, all humming along like well-greased machine parts, one worker as easily replacing a worn-out or damaged part as the next.

Despite tales to the contrary, slaves were not secure in the Old South. The master could rape the slave, beat the slave, or cripple him. And when the master died, his heirs, fighting over the slaves like vultures, could split up the slaves' children to suit the needs of the property settlement. Security in today's workplace is an equally deluding fiction spoken to the frightened heart. *Security is the sweet sister of death.* It wraps its arms around us, lulls us, and cuddles us into sleepy narcotic waves of apathy. Its price is the waste of the person, which leaves his perfect uniqueness imprisoned in some dank cellar called "the secure job," where it remains to rot.

Listen to an old slave master:

What I mean by a perfect understanding between a master and a slave is that the slave should know that his master is to govern absolutely, and he is to obey implicitly. That he is never for a moment to exercise his will . . .

Ask most workers if they are entitled to think, to create, to grow on the job. We know, of course, the Japanese paradigm copied today by some of the more enlightened American companies—the fiction of the friendly family; the encouragement of workers to drop their ideas in the idea box; small groups working, thinking, creating together. But has there ever been a better form of slavery? The corporate master is as incapable of appreciation as it is incapable of any other human feeling. Ask any worker if he owns even a tiny fraction of his invention. Ask the worker if he ever got 1 percent of the money he saved the company from his discovery of a better way. The bonus went to the CEO, who got rich on the stock options given him as a reward for producing a better profit picture for the company.

Security? How could we want security? Here is how the best of the slave masters saw the security of his slave:

The man [the slave] feels confident that the master will only require what is right of him and will abundantly provide for all his wants and that of his family. When he or his children are sick, he knows that he will have his master's physician to minister to him. When he is naked, he knows he will be clothed; and when he is old, he knows that his wants will all be supplied to him in his small cottage; during winter he will be warmed by his master's fire and clothed from his master's flock; and at all times he knows that he will be fed from his master's crib and meat house. The man looks even beyond death and knows that when he shall have died he will be decently buried and his children after him provided for.

Surely we can understand that security masks the reality of slavery—life without life, death while still breathing.

THE LAW OF THE MIRROR

Yet, curiously, the bargain is equally destructive of the master. Slavery reduces the master to a brute. The child born as a slave lives a life of dejection and pain. But the child born as a master lives a false life, one of empty loftiness and cruelty. Who is more to be pitied—the child born to be whipped, or the once-innocent child who will grow up with the whip in his hand? Who is more the lost soul—the slave with frightened eyes, or the blind bigot who believes he performs God's will when he enslaves his fellow man?

The law of slavery calls up *the law of the mirror*. When the slave is chained to the master, the master is chained as well. When the slave is beaten, the master is also reduced, and his arrogance leaves him dull and stupid. And when the master discards his workers, he frees both master and slave without intending to do so.

Today, the downsizing corporation, itself enslaved by the bottom line, frees its workers with its pink slips. At the same time it also unwittingly teaches workers the truth—that the only security is the *security of the self*. I say there is more security in the swamps than in the slave quarters. And should we, too, become bottom-line gazers, we shall discover that whenever the worker is worth a dollar to the corporation in profit, he can be worth two dollars in profit to himself.

Still, I think of the great pain of good men and women who have devoted their lives to the false promises of security and one day awaken to find the infamous pink slip in their hands. But the pain is the pain of slavery. In the end I say, yes! Free us! Drive us from those ugly places of false promises. Drive us out of those dreary holes where we are machines, not men; benumbed automatons, not women.

As another corporation downsizes, John Farrell, head of Chase's human resources department, says, "I can't imagine any corporate entity owing anyone a career." He is right. But the other side of that equation he leaves unsaid: one cannot imagine an honest corporation promising anyone a career expressly or by inference and, at will, breaking the promise. But many corporate managers acknowledge that promises of security are but useful tools in the service of profit, and that they may also be broken in the service of profit.

Despite John Farrell's shrug of the shoulders at the idea of career promises, corporations do promise careers. The corporate structure itself is founded on the workers' critical need for security—workers who will devote their lives to the corporate journey. The corporation entices the young, the eager, and holds up those at the top as role models. It extols success as "upward mobility" in the corporate hierarchy. It establishes goals, both for the worker and the corporation. The golden carrot it dangles is career advancement even over economic betterment.

Although John Farrell's statement is like an arrogant spit in the faces of the lifelong loyal employees who were given such promises, it again activates *the law of the mirror*: I, too, can no more imagine a corporate entity owing anyone a career than I can imagine anyone devoting his life to such a soulless fiction as a corporation. The law of the mirror always prevails. When the master provides security, both master and slave are enslaved. When the master discards the slave, both are liberated. The road to freedom as well as to slavery always runs both ways.

THE UNION OF MANY

The idea of a union of workers has always existed as a force against the tyranny of the powerful. Even in the antebellum South there persisted a sort of unionized slavery; that is to say, the demands made upon the slaves were limited, not out of love for them, but to prevent them from running to the swamps and engaging in work stoppages and protests, all of which proved great nuisances to the masters. Under this "organization of labor" slaves were said to work better. The amount of work expected was set by custom at some plantations, and the planters who adhered to these standards claimed that the amount of work should not be increased much since "there is danger of a general stampede to the 'swamp'—a danger the slave can always hold before his master's cupidity."

But unions today can become but another hole into which the frightened worker can scurry and hide. Unions are no longer a brotherhood or sisterhood. Today, the best union is often but another bad corporation. And today's unions, in most part, have become but another depository for the workers' own liberty.

Often at the union's head the gross, the crooked, the sold-out, and the ignorant speak for the workers in one gravelly voice. How can they who make under-the-table bargains, load up their own silky pockets, and often betray the workers provide the workers with security?

Unions in the days of the robber barons were the working-man's only hope. But already we have forgotten how the rank and file fought shoulder to shoulder. They fought against brazen serfdom—the children laboring in the factories, the mothers bone weary, the fathers beaten down, hungry, and hopeless after the twelve-hour day. They fought against the master's police, who beat them and murdered them, and against the master's courts, which hung them. They fought for their lives, and they stood and bled and died together.

We have forgotten their blood. Instead, today, workers have abdicated their power to the white-collar men of organized labor, those who wear pin-striped suits indistinguishable from the suits worn by their counterparts in management and who would sit as comfortably on the other side of the table. Today's union is but one corporation engaged in its fight for power against yet another corporation, the managers of both reaping the principal spoils of the battle.

THE UNION OF ONE

The new and most powerful union of all will be a *union of one*—one man, one woman, one worker with special skills, an inquiring mind, an independent attitude, with creativity intact and love of life blooming. The *union of one* will be peopled by one man or one woman who is *alive*. And such an alive person is always the great find of every intelligent manager.

In the new-age workplace the master will no longer be the master. The worker will be his own master. He will enter the place of work voluntarily to do a job for a price, *his* price. He will leave as he chooses. He will cherish his freedom, which is his security. He cannot be lured into the trap. The master cannot own him. This one man belongs to the *union of one*, is owned by no one, and represents only himself.

The new-age worker, belonging to the *union of one*, has made himself an expert in whatever job he or she undertakes. Perhaps today he is employed as a baggage handler for the airlines. But he does his work with an expertise that brings order and efficiency to the task. He works to satisfy himself, not the master. But he is also a fry cook because he takes great pleasure in cooking. He can go to work on any day at any restaurant.

She may have acquired one great and always-growing skill, as in the case of those enamored of electronics. But she can work for herself as easily as for her corporate employer. She is not glued to the corporate tit. She may have followed her Renaissance nature and become both writer and editor, both draftsman and artist. He may be a mountain guide as well as a designer of *mountain clothes* and *skateboards*. He may be a ski bum and a forester. She has followed her dreams. Explored the self. Found the bounteous treasures within. Loved them. Cherished them. Kept them and sold them dear. He has time to become a father. She has reserved to the self the most important days of all—the days when she is a mother.

The time is upon us when America will return to the mentality of the artisan, the attitude of the individual craftsman. Workers will again become independent—and own their own tools. I see it already. The cameraman for network television, an independent contractor, brings his own camera to the news scene, does his work, takes his camera home, and goes scuba diving the rest of the day.

Because the new-age workers have been freed to engage in what brings them joy and because they are an independent lot, they are respected. Coveted as workers, they are self-starting, intelligent, and involved, *and they create*. They can find new ways! More profitable ways. They are not plodding drudges in old ruts. They have pride—pride in themselves, which engenders pride in their work. But they will be gone in the morning if they are not treated fairly, if they are not happy, if they cannot create, if they are not appropriately appreciated, and the new-age employer respects them for it.

The new-age member of the *union of one* and Henry David Thoreau would have understood each other: "Simplicity, simplicity, simplicity! I say, let our affairs be as two or three, and not a hundred or a thousand . . . simplicity of life and elevation of purpose." And what higher purpose in life could there be than to do a good day's work when one pleases and, when one pleases, to toss a fly out on a ripple?

In the new-age workplace, the engineer, the draftsman, the computer wizard, the designer, every professional and every skilled artisan, yes, a skilled ditch digger as well, can belong to the new *union of one*. The union dues are free. And the *union of one* will represent them honestly. The union head cannot be bought off. If management doesn't meet the *union of one's* demands, its members can go on strike in the same way that today's corporations, exercising their power, threaten to replace all striking workers with docile, fully obedient workers. If the employer does not meet the demands of the *union of one*, the new-age worker can replace the employer—like *that!*—with a more intelligent, more responsive one—one that better suits the taste and the need of the new-age worker.

Although most employers do not yet understand the truth of it, the free man, and the liberated woman with an alert, creative mind, are the most valuable of all workers, and, at last, cost the employer less even though such workers are paid more. The most valuable worker for the corporation is the worker who no longer demands all of the spangles and sparkles of security that soon dim—the pensions, the benefits that somehow end up enslaving rather than freeing.

The old way has become a dismal game in which both master and slave, chained to each other, hate one another, each fighting the other with their respective weapons—the master with his bullying power, the slave with his aggressive passivity. The worker, seeking security, like the slave of old, does not seek to *do* work but to *avoid* work. The employer, on the other hand, has an opposite goal—to extract as much labor from the worker as can be squeezed from the human body. The worker's goal is not to live at work but to become embalmed during the working day and to lie in the company's casket until quitting time when the quitting bell resurrects him. Then, exhausted and despondent, he is ready for his just deserts—not the sense of a day well spent, but a beer at the tavern with the other part-time corpses who are his fellow workers and friends: "This Bud's for you."

The worker who seeks security cannot exhibit the free mind necessary to spring ahead on his own. He requires an overseer, a time clock, rules of work, rules of vacations, rules of sick leave, rules about having babies, rules about rules. He requires laws to protect him, and commissions to hear his complaints and representatives to represent him. It takes endless paper and energy, and the ugly wrestling deadens the spirit of both master and slave and leaves them both weary and both full of hate.

Wars ought never be fought in the workplace. But today both sides, labor and management alike, have become entrenched in war. When wars are fought in the workplace, there is no respect—not for either side; no caring—not for either side; no pride, no creativity—not for either side; no joy, no sense of having done a job well—not for either side.

THE INTOLERABLE RISK OF SECURITY

The best employment with the best corporation offering the best lifelong security is *at best* a poor bargain. Get out. We must get out—get out if we can. Walk out. Run out. Break down the doors, but get out. The risk is always greater in the slave quarters. The promise of security is but a promise to be broken, and *the risk of security itself is too great*. The risk is that one will live out one's entire life with an anesthetized soul, that one will live out one's whole life as a dead machine in the workplace. To die before one has lived is an unacceptable risk for the living.

When we are free, our minds run free. Perhaps we will see that we must begin our own small business. We cannot know what it is like outside the zoo until we break out. Perhaps we will see that we must go back to school. Trust the freed mind. Freed, it will find the way. Tested, the freed mind will rise up and show itself and find the way. Answers will spring up. They will come flashing before us, bursting from the great fireworks of the liberated brain.

We will, of course, be afraid. How do I feed myself and my family and be free? But fear is the energy of our liberation. And the fear we feel is a fresh, raw fear unclouded and untainted by the fraud and lies of the master. In the end, what price do we place on our new liberty? Are we not rich with it?

FREEING THE MASTER

The worker who is ready to be fired at any moment on any day is the worker who is most valuable to his employer. By being ready to walk off the job, he has kept possession of himself. By possessing the self, he is alert and alive, willing to take risks, to express himself, and to be creative. By shunning security for his freedom, he becomes more valuable to his employer, and, ironically enjoys more security. The horsewhipped, docile sycophant whose best skills are to fawn and snivel will be the first to go when downsizing times come around.

Slavery dulls the master in the same way that it stupefies most slaves. If the new workplace requires a new liberated worker who belongs to the *union of one,* it also requires a new and enlightened employer. How can the master compete in a dynamic world when its managers, its CEOs, swagger and blow in that rare and heady atmosphere, believing themselves to have been enthroned by the gods? Many of these are the great and blustery dupes of business who scurry about in jets, inhabit the golf courses, languish in the plush French restaurants, take home multimillion-dollar bonuses, but, at day's end, don't have the first idea concerning the value or the meaning of their own lives.

THE NEW-AGE MASTER

The new-age business will recognize the worker as the source of its wealth, respect the worker, and provide the worker a place of self-discovery and self-expression. The new-age master that survives in this brutal holocaust of business will share its power with the worker in exchange for the worker's uncommon wisdom. The new-age manager, knowing that the success of the employer must always rest in the hands of the

worker, will provide the worker a fair incentive in the form
of profit sharing, and will aid the worker toward his independence by assisting him in his growth and education, since
the enlightened worker enlightens the workplace.

Former labor secretary Robert Reich said:

> As corporations have focused more and more intensely
> on increasing shareholders' returns and less and less on
> improving the standard of living of their workers, it
> should be no surprise that the stock market has soared
> while pink slips have proliferated and the paychecks of
> most employees have gone nowhere. Do not blame cor-
> porations and their top executives. . . . If we want them
> to put greater emphasis on the interests of their work-
> ers and communities, society must reorganize them to
> do so.

Despite the power of the new-age worker, the corporate
conglomerate, unless reorganized as Reich suggests, will still
be able to afflict whole communities, hurl nations into war,
pollute the entire earth, and destroy the species itself. Suffice
it here to say that as between worker and employer, the new-
age worker will become more aware of his uniqueness and
his value. And he will embrace his freedom as his personal
wealth. At the same time, the new-age corporation will have
abandoned its blind and stupid role as the manipulator and
exploiter, and will have come to realize that its future depends
on a fund of independent, creative workers who will, at last,
free the master.

But I do not endorse the suggested remedy of the former
labor secretary, who wants the tax code rewritten "to reward
companies that promise to avoid layoffs in profitable times

and give their employees a stake in the company, good medical coverage and broad retraining opportunities." Must we bribe corporations with *our* tax money to do what is right— what will, in the long run, enhance corporate profit?

No one pays the worker a bribe to slave for the master. No tax incentives are given the people to struggle in those windowless computer cubicles. No one provides a tax incentive to the three thousand women who are pinioned to their computer monitors in South Dakota fighting deadly boredom until their tendons fail and their wrists give out and their backs grow brittle. Why must we deliver such bribes to the nonpeople to do what is moral, to do what is just and profitable? I say that if any are entitled to a tax incentive, it is those workers who are benumbed by the nature of their labor—workers who should at last be rewarded for their bravery and their endurance.

THE SEVENTH STEP TO FREEDOM: REJECTING THE SLAVERY OF SECURITY

The new-age employer and the new-age worker, supported by the new-age *union of one* will redefine the relationship of worker and employer. The new-age employer will become more of a partner, a supplier of opportunity, an educator, a sharer in dreams, a sharer in profit. The new-age worker will become his own master. He will decide his fate and make and follow his own dreams. He will explore not the master's poisonous caverns of slavery but his own unexplored reaches, in which he will discover his unique self, cherish its value, reject the security of slavery, and encumber his freedom for no one, not even himself.

PART II

FREE AT LAST

Redefining Success

The moral flabbiness born of the exclusive worship of the bitch-goddess SUCCESS. That—with the squalid cash interpretation put on the word success—is our national disease.

—WILLIAM JAMES
1920

THE GUILT OF WEALTH, THE PARADOX OF POVERTY
I bear no affection for socialism. Socialism is merely another face of the same slave master. But let me say it with words as stiff as splinters—the worst enslaving trait of all is greed. I rail against the substitution of money for worth. The idea that the endless accumulation of dead money can furnish a meaningful life to sold-out souls is the supreme lie offered by the system of free enterprise.

One day Imaging, the woman I call my wife but who is the trunk of my tree from which all of my fruit takes bloom, said to me, "Adam"—that is her name for me—"if you feel so guilty about what money we have, give it to the poor and we will live poorly with them. I'll go with you." And she would. That put the issue in perspective. And of my work I thought: what a devilish irony that we who speak loudest for the poor often end up profiting from it.

I do not wish to be poor, not in *any* way poor. Not money-poor, and not poor in the riches of the self. But what rots deepest is greed, the endless appetite for wealth. I do not disparage those with money. I am only opposed to those who, for the sake of acquiring more money, use its power to squeeze yet more of it from the poor.

GREED, THE ULTIMATE VIRTUE?

John Kenneth Galbraith said: "The man who is admired for the ingenuity of his larceny is almost always rediscovering some earlier form of fraud. The basic forms are all known, and have all been practiced. The manners of capitalism improve. The morals may not."

Based on calculations made by the Institute for Policy Studies, the 358 billionaires on this shuddering earth in 1995 possessed a collective wealth of $762 billion, which equaled the income of the poorest *45 percent of all people on the planet.* By 1996 that number blossomed to 447 billionaires, who were worth $1.1 trillion—equal to the income of the earth's poorest 52 percent. *We are speaking of but 447 individuals with wealth equal to approximately 2.5 billion human beings!* At this rate, the wealth of the exclusive billionaires' club will soon equal the annual income of all the other people in the world. Considering a world full of the starving, these calculations provide the most accurate and profound definition of obscenity.

In 1997 Bill Gates, the Microsoft billionaire, more than doubled his net worth, from $18.5 billion to $39.8 billion. It would take the median U.S. household earning $35,000 some 600,000 years to make as much as Gates did in that single year. In 1997 the average worker barely kept up with inflation, while the combined wealth of the *Forbes* 400 increased

31 percent, from $477 billion in 1996 to upwards of $624 billion.

THE DISADVANTAGED RICH — WORMS TO A CORPSE

Yet we should be compassionate, for greed consumes the greedy victims. Consider the rich man who has inherited his wealth. More than likely he grew up as a disadvantaged child. If someone is demented, we call him challenged. I say that the child born rich is also challenged. He will likely never wonder where his next meal will come from, never worry about putting a roof over his head or clothes on his body. Likely he will never be called upon to test the resources of the self, which will atrophy from disuse, and likely he will never be given an opportunity to grow from the struggles most often encountered by the poor. He is likely to turn out as badly as any child in the projects of Chicago. His visions, although different, will likely be as limited and distorted as theirs.

I think of the Menendes brothers, whose values were as shallow as rain on the pavement. They became members of an effete class who are more concerned with how they *look* than with how they *are*—a class held up by the corporate image-makers as superior, the deadpan models in *Gentlemen's Quarterly* who stand for the notion that clothes, not conduct, make the statement, that leisure, fun, fast cars, and fast friends are the mark of success.

I think of the lost Du Pont heir, whose money so deprived him of his chance to become a person that his greatest contribution to mankind was the murder of an innocent athlete. His life was spared only because he was found insane. Must we not pity those whose only claim to personhood is dead money? Which is not to say that wealthy persons cannot become persons, but that persons who are *only* wealthy are, at last, nothing at all.

Said de Tocqueville as early as 1840:

Nothing is quite so wretchedly corrupt as an aristocracy which has lost its power but kept its wealth and which still has endless leisure to devote to nothing but banal enjoyments. All its great thoughts and passionate energy are things of the past, and nothing but a host of petty, gnawing vices now cling to it like worms to a corpse.

A NEW PARADIGM FOR SUCCESS

The new paradigm for success in America must be *person-based,* not *money-based.* A successful person is one who has acquired, not great wealth, but *great personhood.* The wealthy man who has not become a person is only an empty sack powered by churning greed. The individual who has achieved personhood is a lily in perpetual bloom. The paradigm of wealth as virtue, of money as success, of profit as the ultimate human goal, is the most enslaving value of all.

According to the current standard of success, the successful man can squeeze still more interest from the poor and ignore the hungry children, and if he has become rich enough, even at the pain of millions of helpless people, he will be admired. We know him—the man who, having been crowned by money, exhorts the world to bow down in its worship and his. He can buy whatever engages his fancy—the fifty-thousand-square-foot palace often done in garish taste; the long penile automobiles that may be in compensation for his impotence; the women who, impelled by the same passion for money, find its power obscenely seductive. I never knew an ugly rich person, man or woman, who could not secure one of the opposite sex who, ostensibly, appears beautiful.

Recently I was talking with a young female producer about this subject. A well-known personality with mountains of money who walked with a toddle and who was old enough to be his bride's grandfather had just married a pretty young woman. He was reputed to have the personality of a guppy.

"How can this happen?" I asked the producer. "What could she possibly see in the man?"

"She sees his money."

"I know," I said. "That's obvious. But how can the money attract her?"

The young woman looked at me as if I were a newborn idiot. "Money is a powerful aphrodisiac," she said, dreamy eyed and distant, her voice suddenly husky. Yet take away this man's money, and put a waiter's apron on him, or a pair of workman's gloves, and he could not hold a job or a conversation.

I think of the men who have slaved for the corporate master, sacrificing their lives as foremen, executives, and CEOs. Then they retire and go to their reward—those air-conditioned adobe affairs at some Arizona retirement village on a golf course. Robert Menzies, an Australian prime minister, once remarked:

A man may be a tough, concentrated, successful money-maker and never contribute to his country anything more than a horrible example. A manager may be tough and practical, squeezing out, while the going is good, the last ounce of profit and dividend, and may leave behind him an exhausted industry and a legacy of in-

dustrial hatred. A tough manager may never look outside his own factory walls or be conscious of his
partnership in a wider world. I often wonder what
strange cud such men sit chewing when their working
days are over, and the accumulating riches of the mind
have eluded them.

I think of the phenomenon as the completed circle, from
cradle to coffin. No longer do we behold a satin-lined crib,
but a satin-lined casket. The helpless babe has been ex-
changed for the stiffened corpse. The family, the friends, drop
by to pay their last respects. The thought must come to their
minds, "What does his life stand for?" It stands for a hundred
million dollars, no doubt. It stands for workers squeezed dry
like empty sponges. It stands for endless haggles over money,
profit, the battles for a never-sufficient market share. It stands
for countless hostilities with unions and consumer battles.
Perhaps it stands for a useful product given to the public at
a price not that the public can afford, but that the competi-
tion permits. In the end, the life was successful according to
current standards. He had money, and because of it he had
respect. At the same time I think of van Gogh, who was never
able to sell a painting and who remains immortal.

"MAN, THAT'S LIVIN' "

I remember the old story of the man who wanted to be buried
in his gold-plated Cadillac—for him the ultimate symbol of
success. The crane is at the grave site; the Cadillac is being
hoisted up over the waiting hole; the deceased is fully dressed
in his tuxedo, sitting erect, his hands affixed to the wheel. As
corpse and car are being lowered into the abyss, two grave
diggers sitting on top of the pile of excavated dirt are watch-

ing the whole affair. Suddenly one of them shakes his head in wonderment and says to the other, "Man, that's livin'!"

THE NEW "SUCCESSFUL PERSON"

I repeat, I am not speaking against the notion of free enterprise. Men should be at liberty to engage in whatever enterprise they choose. I am not suggesting that we impose much of a limitation on the greedy. The greedy should be free to be nearly as greedy as they wish. Their neurosis, so long as it does not threaten the right of their neighbors to exist, is their neurosis, and they must struggle either to incessantly feed it or to cure themselves of it. I am speaking of *our* view of success. I am speaking about whom we should endow with *our* respect. I am speaking about a new archetype of the "successful person."

In the Middle Ages as today, money was necessary because without it, absent barter, man could not support himself and his family or help his needy neighbor. But the goal of material riches was secondary. Riches existed for man, not man for riches. In the Middle Ages it was acceptable for a man to seek such wealth as was necessary, but to seek more was avarice, and avarice was a mortal sin.

Beyond the needs of the businessman, the business of business was to be carried on for the public good, and the profits he took were not to be more than the value of his own labor. Controls were not imposed by the system against the greedy. There was a common value among the people that scorned the likes of our modern capitalist, whose overriding goal is the acquisition of money, and more money—money without end, Amen. In short, greed, as viewed by our Middle Age forebears, was rejected as a virtue, and loathed as a vice.

But by the late Middle Ages that system of values began

to change, and by the sixteenth century it had collapsed. Monopolies began to spring up. The following words from Luther's small pamphlet *On Trading and Usury* are as relevant today as when he first wrote them:

> They [the monopolies] have all commodities under their control and practice without concealment all tricks that have been mentioned; they raise and lower prices as they please and oppress and ruin all the small merchants, as they pike the little fish in the water, just as though they were lords over God's creatures and free from all the laws of faith and love.

In the Middle Ages, when a moral power was prevalent, success was defined in terms of morality. When monopolies took over, power shifted, so that by the sixteenth century success had become redefined in terms of wealth.

Today money is seen as the unquestionable symbol of power. And our view of success is therefore principally measured in money. In general terms, those who have money are successful. Those who do not are not. Even in today's slightly camouflaged slave state, those who have money, although they may be slaves themselves, are held up as successful. Those who do not have money are the lowest of the slaves, and are not seen as successful. Although we give lip service to Mother Teresa and recognize her success as a person, and although we may acknowledge Martin Luther King, Jr., as a successful human being, few strive to emulate either. When Princess Diana and Mother Teresa died during the same week, the fantasies of the masses were ignited by the rich and the sexy, not the poor and the saintly.

There remains a paucity of courses in our colleges that

teach us how to become *successful persons* but many teach us how to make money, how to conduct business, how to beat the law in courts of justice, and how to convert ourselves into commodities so that we may sell ourselves in the labor market for money and therefore become "successful."

THE *APPEARANCE* OF MONEY

Money or the appearance of money stands for nearly every virtue in America. If we have money, at least enough of it to buy a meal at a fancy restaurant, and if we can comply with the dress code of a jacket and a tie, we may join the others in the dining room, all of whom appear to be equally mon-eyed and successful. Said Thoreau, "It is an interesting question how far men would retain their relative rank if they were divested of their clothes." And Thoreau again: "I say, beware of all enterprises that require new clothes, and not rather a new wearer of clothes."

Recently several of us approached the maître d' in a Chicago restaurant for a table. The maître d', with feigned sorrow, said he could not seat us. "The jeans, you know." He pointed at mine with a certain puckered lemon look on his face.

"May I ask you a question," I said.

"Of course," he said, his nose tilted.

"If Jeffrey Dahlmer came in here—you know, the killer who liked to eat his victims—and he was wearing the required coat and tie, sans jeans, would you seat him?"

"I suppose," he said.

"What would you do if Jesus Christ came in wearing jeans?"

"I hope you will come back," he said. It was the proper thing to say.

Appearance, of course, is not a good substitute for propriety. Yet a snooty world loves its pretenses. Thin garb covers deep deficiencies.

I know a man who is nearly eighty years old. Let us call him Sam Superficial. He dyes his gray hair red. He has had his nose reshaped and retextured. He wears expensive clothes, married a woman young enough to be his granddaughter, drives a Rolls, and wears a heavy gold watch that, along with a diamond the size of a hen's egg, must each day absorb a major portion of his bodily energy to lug around. I asked him, "Sam, what is all of this show of affluence about?"

"Why," he replied incredulously, "I have to make a *statement.*"

"A statement? What do you mean, a statement?"

"Why, a statement—as to who I *am*," he said.

"Well," I asked, "who are you?" There was a long silence. Then he finally said, "You know who I am," and he laughed and patted me on the back.

How we look! I rarely go into a group of people without hearing many say, as if out of habit, "You're *looking* good," which is this culture's substitute for saying anything substantive at all. If you *look* all right, you must *be* all right. If you *look* successful, you must *be* successful. If you look like others look, you must be one of them, a member of the club, and therefore all right.

If your clothes are expensive, you must have good taste and therefore be a tasteful person. When clients come to my office and find the attorneys there attired in sweatshirts and jeans, they are likely put off for the moment. Power suits with power pinstripes are the uniform of success. You can dress an idiot to the teeth, and he is still an idiot. But a lawyer in his office who, in comfortable clothes, is laboring for the rights of his clients can more easily call upon his creative energies when none of those energies are focused on how he looks. In such a profession, one needs every assistance to *be* competent, rather than to *appear* competent. I never saw a fancy suit that could take the place of a well-thought-out argument.

In America, success, being but another commodity that may be purchased, requires merely that we grasp enough of it to don the trappings of the wealthy. You know the silly old saw: "Money talks. Bullshit walks." I say, money talks, and it's mostly bullshit.

Most of the wealthy persons I know have, in the pursuit of the dollar, lost their ability to see value elsewhere. I cannot remember ever having met a wealthy man who was a poet. Most have not read a poem in thirty years. Large numbers of the "successful businessmen" with whom I am acquainted know something about golf and the condition of their fellow golfers' handicap. But they know little about the condition of their workers as they struggle to put their children through school, or of the multitudes of those workers they have laid off as part of a much-praised downsizing. The champion moneymaker is viewed as highly intelligent and will adorn the cover of *Time* magazine when, in truth, he may simply be lucky and cruel.

Although a person may become a person despite the fact that he has made large sums of money, still nothing is more destructive of personhood—indeed, of success—than money itself. Although it is conducive to personhood to have food in the belly and a roof overhead, five-thousand-dollar suits, a pearl-colored Lamborgini, and a beach nymph on each arm do not promote personhood. Once we accept the acquisition of large sums of money as equivalent to success, we have made the fatal judgment.

If you have money, you can join the Valley Country Club. If you do not, even if you are a Nobel Prize winner and have given all of your prize money to charity, you may not be welcome. If you have money, even if you are evil at heart and so greedy you would cheat the maid out of an hour on Christmas day, you will be greeted with open arms by the church to which you have made a large, loudly advertised contribution.

I remember when we visited St. Peter's in Rome. The cathedral is so huge you could take off in a small plane over the length of the marble floors. I watched the tourists as they exited. The people passed by nuns who held out bowls in support of that great historical structure, and the people dropped their money in the bowls. But they turned their heads from the wretched beggars who, on the steps of the cathedral, extended their empty hands for a penny. Money given into the hands of the church was the way to salvation. Money given into the hands of beggars was a waste.

THE ENSLAVEMENT OF MONEY

Money in doses hugely disproportionate to our needs enslaves. Man's search must not be for dead money. Man's search must take place in the long, winding corridors of the self. How could one lay one's head down upon the embalming bed without having explored every niche and alcove, every attic and basement, for the bonanza that is hidden in the self? It is as if a miser lived in the most wondrous botanical garden filled with every fragrant plant and flower, every blooming tree and shrub, every bearing bush and vine, in which the birds sing and the wild deer roam. In possession of such a garden, the miser sits in the cellar with his green visor pulled down low over his eyes. Over and over he counts his crumpled bills, a stranger to himself and wasted to the world until his yellowed corpse is hauled off, after which his body will, for the first time, touch the earth.

In 1863, Thoreau writing in *Life Without Principles,* saw it thus: "Business!" he exclaimed. "I think there is nothing, not even crime, more opposed to poetry, to philosophy, ay, to life itself, than this incessant business. . . . There is no more fatal blunder than he who consumes the greater part of his life getting his living." And in *Walden* he wrote: "Why should we be in such a desperate haste to succeed and in such desperate enterprises? If a man does not keep pace with his companions, perhaps it is because he hears a different drummer." Finally the sage of the woods said it all: "However mean your life is, meet it and live it; do not shun it and call it hard names. . . . Cultivate poverty like a garden herb, like sage."

MONEY AND FREEDOM

I say that when one is too long in the presence of mere dead money, one is likely to catch the fatal disease. I have never seen a thing grow that is planted in money. Yet money is a useful tool, and it takes a quantum of money in this money-society to free one's self. The great works of the Renaissance likely would never have graced the domes but for the money of patrons. Michelangelo might never have created his masterpieces without the support of the Medici family. Much of the immortal music and the classical literature we so cherish might never have sprung from the souls of their creators but for the stipends of the wealthy. But the artists were liberated not to pursue money but to pursue themselves. Today one needs to become one's own patron to free the artist within.

I see the struggle everywhere among those gifted in the arts. I see musicians struggling to feed their bodies as they fight to free the muse. I see young painters unable to loose the angels, to affix their extraordinary visions to their canvases. Mountain climbers, half-starved and ragged, endure the pain of poverty to touch the tops of peaks. Poets wither away on park benches, or along desolate, lonely roads. I know whole crowds of talented people. I know a bucking horse rider who works between rodeos in the hay fields, and a marathon runner who works nights as a bellman. Yet sometimes the struggle itself lends itself to a better journey through the self. I doubt that but for van Gogh's struggle we would have known his exquisitely tortured art. One thinks of the piteous waste if van Gogh, living today, were to sell himself as a commercial artist to create an ad page for Ralph Lauren's toggies.

SHEDDING MONEY FOR SUCCESS

In America success has become a painful, endless, enslaving quest for money. But success must, in the end, be measured not by others, but by ourselves. Carnegie cruelly stole the lives of thousands of workers to amass his fortune. But I daresay, until he gave it away to found the nation's libraries, he was not a success, especially not to himself. Rockefeller took his fortune from the earth, and from the backs of the people, but until he contributed a portion of his wealth to the establishment of his charities, he was not a success to himself.

UNSUNG SAINTS

On the other hand, one need not be a Mother Teresa or a Martin Luther King, Jr., to be successful. I know men who by virtue of being successful fathers have achieved a success far beyond the riches of the magnate whose usual effort as a father is to hire a nanny when his children are young and to shuttle them off to an expensive boarding school when they become troublesome teenagers. Such a man believes he can purchase everything, including his fatherhood. Still, in praise of the paradox, although money is no substitute for fatherhood, in moderate doses it has proven to be a good thing for the health of the family.

I know women who have risen above the saints by reason of their motherhood. No artist's masterpiece can match a mother's creation of a successful child, one who has been freed to explore and to grow. Who is more laudable—a land developer who takes a piece of raw and beautiful valley, cuts it up, creates shopping malls and golf courses, and builds those expensive houses around the fairways for the rich, and who thereby becomes rich himself; or a poor mother who struggles to feed and dress her child, who nurtures him with love, opens his being to the boundless possibilities of life, and thereby produces a *person?* Success is measured not only by who we are, but by what gifts we give. As the old chief said, "The gift is not complete until it is given again." Ah, the mother whose gift to the world is a *person!*

MONEY, THE ERRONEOUS INVESTMENT

By the end of the Middle Ages the desire for wealth had become an all-absorbing passion. Martin Butzer, a preacher of the late Middle Ages, complained:

> All the world is running after those trades and occupations that will bring the most gain. . . . All the clever heads, which have been endowed by God with a capacity for the nobler studies, are engrossed by commerce,

which nowadays is so saturated with dishonesty that it is the last sort of business an honorable man should engage in.

Christ probably said it best: "For what shall it profit a man if he shall gain the whole world, and lose his own soul?"

The "time is money" rule is one that converts life to dollars, which is the cruelest fraud of all. I know a plastic surgeon who figures his time is worth a thousand dollars an hour. One day I asked him, "Do you ever 'stop to smell the roses'?"

"How long?" he asked, as we hurried by a sidewalk garden.

"Say, a minute," I replied.

"My time is worth a thousand an hour," he said. Then, as if he were a walking calculator, he said, "It would cost me sixteen dollars and sixty-six cents a minute to stop and smell the roses. I can buy a whole bouquet for ten bucks from the street vendor on the corner," which would, of course, put him well ahead of the game.

The new paradigm of success must be the amassing of a different and incalculable fortune—the wealth of *becoming a person*. We should be investing in the exploration of the self and in opening the gateway to unexplored frontiers in our children. Ought we not presume the wealthy as presumptively greedy instead of presumptively successful? I would recognize the accomplishment of a man who invents a better mousetrap and becomes wealthy. But such success is measured by his contribution, not by the money he has amassed in the process.

ULTIMATE WEALTH

Jean Jacques Rousseau, the man who more than any other influenced the Founding Fathers, believed in the freedom of the human spirit. That enlightened notion echoed throughout the language of the Declaration of Independence and the Constitution itself—the right to life, liberty, and the pursuit of happiness. The desire of the founders was to be free of the despotism of convention. To them, the tyranny of politically correct thinking would have been a horror. Their dream was of a nation in which the rights and dignity of the individual flowered in every season, especially the right to unfettered thought. Yet, as today, their success was largely founded on the backs of their slaves.

To be sure, the pursuit of money attracted the attention of the great minds of the time. Jefferson, facing bankruptcy, put his slaves to the manufacture of nails to gain a profit. But the primary archetype of success was not the gross accumulation of wealth, but public service, which, ironically, was in large part made possible by the slave labor of thousands of helpless men and women born in shackles. Rousseau said: "It is too difficult to think nobly when one thinks only of earning a living."

The false symbols of success disguise the person beneath. They cover the evil, the tawdry, the insensitive and mundane, with what are today socially acceptable symbols of success— the Rolls Royce, at least the new Jag, the jet with the gold-plated latrine, the fifteen-bedroom guest house on the beach, and a $12,450 Kisselstein-Cord "large trophy" handbag. The trappings of wealth are the costumes of players who refuse to show themselves, who show only their exterior masks, the phony furnishings that leave hidden the shriveled, lonely, often piteous and neurotic creature beneath.

And how will we come to adopt a new paradigm of success? Rousseau offered the solution. The solution lies in the riskiest of all activities, education—risky because it creates the image of possibility, and such an image always precedes change. Rousseau said, "All that we lack at birth, all that we need when we come to man's estate, is the gift of education."

Education will bring on a time when we shall see a mother who has taught her daughter to dance to the music of the self as more valuable than the broker who played the stock market from the inside and now owns half of the good ranch land in Wyoming, which he hordes for his private fishing.

Education will bring on a time when we shall see a father who has taught his son that true wealth is derived from investing in the self as more valuable than the investment banker who, having arranged the financing of yet another gambling extravaganza in Las Vegas, shaves off millions for his own account.

Education will bring on a time when we shall see the poor man who flings himself in front of the oncoming bulldozers to protect the trees as more valuable than the corporate executive who has elevated the stock of his company by stripping the land bare of forest and shipping millions of unsawed logs to Japan.

One day, when education has performed its magic, we shall see the unmasked, open faces of people who are proud of *who* they have become, not of the clothes they wear, the clubs they belong to, or the possessions behind which they hide their diminished selves.

MONEY, THE PARENT OF SLAVES

Success, then, must be redefined: Our American notion of success, which is inextricably tied to money, is the enslaving deceit that causes the species to give up life in exchange for that which contains no life at all. Our money-driven view of success causes us to bow our necks in the traces to acquire it, to sell ourselves to our masters to possess it, to become slaves in order to be seen by our fellow slaves as successful.

Slavery and money are copulating twins, the progeny of which is the empty man.

If we exist in an enslaving money system—one in which we exchange our lives for money—a formula for achieving our freedom in such a system can be easily constructed: *The less of one's life one must exchange for money, the more freedom one may enjoy.*

On the one hand, this formula grants the most freedom to the born rich, whose only effort to achieve money is to clip the coupon, and, on the other, to the homeless, who by choice sleep under the fire escape and whose only possessions are contained in the small pack on their backs. I do not envy such freedom at either extreme.

But the formula in this raw money society is worth working with. If we own a home valued at $150,000 and we have a mortgage on it for $120,000 for 30 years at 8 percent, and if we own a car that we purchased for $20,000 with interest at 10 percent for 5 years, and, trading in the old model, we buy a new car every 5 years, and if we have an average credit card balance of $5,000 on which we pay interest at 18 percent each year, these combined interest payments alone, starting when we are 25 and ending when we are 65, will amount to something like $223,987.23. If we are working for a wage of $30,000 a year, we will contribute *7.47 years of our precious lives to the bank*— just to pay their interest. And that is over slavery.

WE, THE NEW INDIANS

Sometimes I wonder if we are not the new Indians who have given up our land and our freedom and are imprisoned upon the master's reservation in our small concrete condos and deadly boring jobs in exchange for the master's firewater and beads. How much more of our lives must we deliver to the master for his trinkets; his TV dinners; his entertainment; the subscriptions to his pay television; his packaged vacations; his designer clothes; his toiletries, which are sold to us to make us smell better and look younger; his endless appliances; his Cokes and his Pepsis with their sugar and caffeine to give us false energy to get through the deadly day; his beer, which we are told we deserve at the end of the slave's work; his cigarettes, which we are told give us freedom but which provide us, instead, with the joy of heart disease and cancer?

SURVIVING TO CONSUME

"Work to survive, survive by consuming, survive to consume: the hellish cycle is complete," cried the Belgian philosopher Raoul Vaneigem. I think of the conversation I recently had with a man named Fisher. Fisher was after Nora about her coffee again. She runs a small café near where I live.

"My heirs are going to sue you, Nora," he said. He turned to me. "Spence here will represent them."

"What are ya talkin' about?" Nora asked.

"This coffee of yours would kill anybody. My heirs are gonna sue."

"Your heirs are gonna give me a bonus," she said, filling his cup. He lifted the cup and sniffed the steam. Then he took a sip and turned to me. Something was on his mind. "Things aren't like they used to be," he said.

"That's for sure," I said.

He had a faraway look in his eyes. "Used to be you didn't need all the crap they sell you."

"What's the matter?" I asked. "Betts"—that's his wife—"want a new can opener or something?" Fisher was penurious. Ran his house like his business.

"No. She wants a new toaster oven."

"What do they cost?"

"About seventy-five bucks."

"You got seventy-five million, and you don't want to spend seventy-five bucks?"

"You don't get seventy-five million by spending seventy-five bucks," he said. "She's already got one of those two-oven stoves. She's got a friggin' toaster. She's got one of those fancy microwaves. Jesus. When does it stop?"

Then he launched into the monolog I'd heard twenty times before. "This whole country is fucked up," he began. "When I was a kid, my mother stayed home. My old man worked for City Plumbing. We lived in an old house in Jersey City, and she raised a garden. Had a few chickens. Made our clothes. Canned the vegetables out of the garden. Made the bread. Jesus Christ, it was good bread. None of that soggy bakery stuff that mold won't grow on. If mold won't grow on the bread, it's poison."

"Right," I said. "We used to buy day-old bread for eight cents a loaf because it was moldy. My mother trimmed off the mold and said nobody would know the difference. But I knew the difference."

"Now Betts wants a friggin' toaster oven. For fucking what? That's what the stove oven is for. She's got two of 'em."

"Not as handy," I said.

"There you go! That's it! When I was a kid, we didn't have any double ovens, and the toast got toasted. We didn't have a microwave, and our food got cooked. You buy that frozen shit, and you got to have a microwave. The women can't cook anymore. They go out and bust their asses all day at some nine-to-five job and let microwaves cook the Salisbury steak. They could have stayed home in the first place, cooked a better meal for half the money. Now she wants a friggin' toaster oven, and she doesn't even work."

"You want her to work?"

"I want her to stay home. I do the work. Nora," he hollered across the room, "give me another shot of that rotgut."

"Why have her stay home if you come down here to Nora's for breakfast every morning?"

"She can't cook."

"Maybe if she had a toaster oven she could."

"She couldn't cook if I bought her a nuclear reactor. When I was a kid, my mother washed on Mondays and ironed on Tuesdays. No fancy automatic washer—one of those old jobs where you had to be careful not to get yer tit in the wringer. But nobody was suing in those days. She hung out the clothes to dry. Clothespins and all—you know. No electric dryers. We had one old car. No payments. The house was old. Running toilet. Old man a plumber." He laughed. Sometimes his laugh was the kind that did not allow you to laugh back. "Now she wants a friggin' toaster oven."

"Who's the boss at your house?" I knew how to get Fisher going.

"I'll tell you one thing: my mother did it all. Stayed home and took care of the kids. No day care. No crime. Never had to lock the fucking door at night. Those were the days. Now a wife gets up screaming. Gotta get the kids dressed and to school. They don't get a decent breakfast. They eat some greasy junk food on the way, and they get dumped off at the day care with a bunch of snotty little bastards. The kid's always sick. Then the parents get sick. I tried to tell my daughter to stay home and take care of her kids. But all she wants to do is make money."

"Chip off the old block, I'd say."

"Hell of a good publicist. Works for the biggest firm in L.A. Never see her. Never see the grandkids." When Fisher looked sad like that, it made you want to say something nice to him.

"You must miss 'em," I said.

"My daughter doesn't know her kids. 'What do you want all that money for?' I asked her. 'When your kids are grown up, all you're going to have is a shitpot full of money in the bank and kids you never met.' "

"What did she say?" I asked.

"She says I should know." He started talking to the wall. "Christ, if she stayed home, she could probably save as much as she makes and have her kids too. But the women nowadays don't want to do housework. Too good for housework." Then he said to me, "My mother wasn't too good for housework. My daughter is always going to her shrink. If she did the wash on Monday and the ironing on Tuesday, she wouldn't need to go to the fuckin' shrink every Wednesday night. A little work takes care of all that mental health crap. My mother was happy."

"How do you know?"

"She never complained about a fuckin' thing. But my daughter . . . Jesus!" he said. He was shaking his head.

"Does she have a toaster oven?"

"You fuckin' right. She's got everything."

BUYING BACK OUR LIBERTY

Everybody, including Fisher, is right about some things. How much freedom could we buy for ourselves by keeping our own lives, huge chunks of which are delivered to the master for his baubles? How much freedom could we buy if, say, we owned one car instead of two, one TV instead of two? What if we had a small garden and canned our own food, like our mothers used to do? What if we put away the potatoes and carrots and parsnips and turnips in sand in the cellar as our grandparents used to do? What if we entertained ourselves in our own neighborhoods and saw two movies a year instead of twenty? What if all the day care that the family pays for were saved, and the mother or the father, one or both, did at home what they wanted to do most—maybe work as a designer, work with the computer, write, or run an in-house office?

What if we drove the single family car to the mountains and camped out rather than taking a trip to Disneyland or Marine World? What would happen if we canceled the pay TV and all our subscriptions to periodicals and, once a week, as a family, visited the local library? Are we still capable of hanging our clothes out to dry? Of darning a pair of socks or ironing a shirt? For some it would be a source of pleasure. Can we do our own painting, our own home repair work? Can we fix a car or trade housework with a neighbor who can?

I was talking with a carpenter the other day. I asked him what his wife did. He said she took care of the neighbor's kids for a wage and was thereby able to stay at home and take care of her own. Together the carpenter and his wife got by and *kept their kids*. Could we not once more live on the salary of one of the parents? Or on the combined salaries of parents who are employed part-time? How much of our lives could we *buy back* if we cherished our lives instead of our things? How much of our lives could we buy back if our view of success were altered?

And what would happen to the crime rate if America launched into such a program—a new definition of success: a parent at home, the violence of TV shut off, the children learning to garden, to sew, to cook, to discover, to wonder, to explore? Would it be a different world, if, at last we experienced a new success, one in which money became nearly irrelevant, and becoming a person nearly everything?

Free at Last

The idea of freedom seeps up from the core of us. We long for freedom, but the risks—we do not wish to take the risks. Our jobs. Our standing in the community. What if we were voted out of our clubs, or excommunicated from our churches? The fear of it. The deep pain of fear, of facing the unknown—and alone. And what about the threat of the church? To be condemned to an eternal hell, and by a god whom we were assured was a loving god?

What if we had to let go of certain beliefs, deprive ourselves of certain prejudices, and be open to new ideas? Does that not frighten one? And to give up our ideas of success—the money. The power. Is it not easier to accumulate money than to acquire the elusive stuff of personhood? And so I ask, considering the high cost of freedom, do we really want it? It is easier to talk of it—safer. Easier to deny the zoo in which we live, to see beyond the walls as if the walls do not exist.

Yet I say, as someone said before me, "This is no dress rehearsal." We awaken to find ourselves on life's stage, where we "strut and fret" upon it—but once. Are we not the playwrights, the producers, the directors, and the stars? We can, of course, take part in the expected, mundane performance that is dictated to us, that we are comfortable with, that ignores who we are, that is deaf to what we have to say and that bores not only us but all who can muster the energy to watch the dull affair.

Or, coming upon this magical stage this once, this only time, we can perform a magnificent drama, one that discovers who we are, that portrays the struggles, the conflicts, the disappointments, the sorrows, the joys, and satisfactions—yes, perhaps even the victories. Perhaps it is the compelling story of our struggle for freedom itself. Perhaps it is the story of a humble mother working to raise her children to be free, perhaps the story of an inventor, a doctor, a teacher, or a lawyer all attempting to fulfill themselves by making their gifts of self. Perhaps it is the story of a worker who finds his freedom in the workplace and becomes a valuable contributor to his employer and his community. Whatever the story, it will, of course, be yours. You will write the script and play it out. It will be the story of your struggle to be as free as you are able to be—or it can be a different story mumbled from within the confines of the zoo.

As we have seen, none of us are ever fully free. As long as others inhabit the world, we must, of course, temper our lives and actions so that they shall have an equal chance at their own freedom. None of us can shed all of the shackles. We shall always bear the tattoos that have been inked on our souls by our experiences, our parents, and our genes. But at our cores an energy moves us to wrest for ourselves as much freedom as we can endure in exchange for the price we must finally pay for it.

Yet some of us will never be satisfied until we have tested

our absolute boundaries. We are the explorers, the nomads who, in times of old, discovered every crack and crevice on the face of the globe, who fought the interminable wilds, the bitter extremes of climate from equator to polar cap, who struggled up the fiercest peaks and sailed across the most dangerous seas. Today, some have set out on an equally exciting adventure—to discover themselves and to experience the world around them. To some, perhaps to you, such an incomparable adventure has become the meaning of life.

The commitment of our lives to the struggle for freedom is the extreme challenge. To be enslaved by ourselves, by others, is an unacceptable form of death. I have heard people exclaim that to be free takes great courage. But does it not take more courage to exist partly dead and to drag the dead parts after us wherever we go? Still, many have borne such a burden for so long they can no longer feel the terrible weight, nor imagine the lightness were those great dead chunks dropped behind.

The purpose of this book has been to invite you to become aware of your inimitable beauty, of your perfection, of your unlimited potential in living free, and of the power each of you has, no matter where you came from and no matter where you find yourself, to one day break free.

When you think of breaking free, think of yourself as one who has been wrongly condemned to prison for life. You can survive the horror of your imprisonment only if you have a plan of escape. You can survive only if you put your plan into action. Perhaps you may do nothing more than dig a single spoonful of dirt each day. Perhaps you will even eat the spoonful each day until your tunnel beneath the walls has finally been dug.

But your devotion to your freedom becomes the meaning

of your life. Then one night you inch through the tunnel to freedom and leave the putrid smell of the prison behind you. Perhaps you experience the perfect joy of freedom for only an hour. But in light of your hopeless imprisonment, that single hour has been worth the long, treacherous struggle— the fresh air, the endless stars, myriad blades of grass under your feet. Or, indeed, you may make your escape good, and enjoy your freedom forever. With all of my heart I wish such freedom for you.

Notes

Recognizing the Slave Within. First appeared in part as chapter 10, "The Slave Within," in *Give Me Liberty: Freeing Ourselves in the Twenty-first Century* (New York: St. Martin's Press, 1998).

Recapturing the Perfect Self. First appeared in part as chapter 9, "Empowering the Self," in *Give Me Liberty,* supra.

Inquisitor of the Self. First appeared in part in chapter 10, "The Slave Within," in *Give Me Liberty,* supra.

Becoming Religiously Irreligious . . . The report of the study of the Agricultural Society of Union District of South Carolina on providing slaves with religion is from *Advice Among Masters,* pp. 237, 238, as is the slave owner's statement about the great civilizer, the cowhide, which is at p. 330. The statement that slavery was ordained in heaven is found at p. 16.

Frederick Douglass's letter to his former master is in *Letters of a Nation: A Collection of Extraordinary American Letters,* edited by Andrew Carroll (Kodansha, 1997), pp. 93–101.

Notes

The Susan Boggs quote is from *American Freedmen's Inquiry Commission Interviews,* 1863, reported in *Slave Testimony,* pp. 419–21.

The quotes concerning the attitude of the church toward slavery came from *Time on the Cross: The Economics of American Negro Slavery,* Robert W. Fogel and Stanley L. Engerman (Boston: Little Brown and Company, 1947).

The claim that the Vatican helped large numbers of Nazis to escape is from *Unholy Trinity: The Vatican, the Nazis, and Soviet Intelligence,* Mark Aarons and John Loftus (New York: St. Martin's Press, 1998).

George Baer's statement was reported by Edward S. Herman, *Corporate Control, Corporate Power* (New York: Cambridge University Press, 1981).

The Ludlow Massacre story can be found in Richard O. Boyer and Herbert M. Morais, *Labor's Untold Story,* 3d ed. (United Electrical Workers, 1982).

The quote from Archbishop Hughes was reported by McPherson in *Battle Cry of Freedom,* p. 507.

Henry Ford's statement are from John Naisbitt and Patricia Aburdene, *Reinventing the Corporation: Transforming Your Job and Your Company for the New Information Society* (New York: Warner Books, 1985) and David Halberstam, *The Reckoning* (New York: William Morrow, 1986).

Smahalla's statement that his young men will never work is from T. C. McLuhan, *Touch the Earth* (New York: Promontory Press, 1971), p. 56.

Notes

Erich Fromm's theory that the anxiety of predestination is responsible for modern man's compulsion to activity is discussed in his *Escape from Freedom* (Henry Holt and Company, 1965), pp. 39–102.

The Magical Power of Aloneness. First appeared in part in chapter 13, "The Power of Aloneness," in *Give Me Liberty,* supra.

Withholding Permission to Lose. First appeared in part in chapter 14, "The Magical Weapon: Withholding Permission to Be Defeated," in *Give Me Liberty,* supra.

Rejecting the Slavery of Security. The quote from a master concerning the machinery-like aspect of managing his slaves is from Breeden, *Advice Among Masters,* p. 31, as is the statement that the slave should never exercise his will, which is at p. 30. The slave master's view of security is from pp. 8 and 9.

The quote from John Farrell concerning a corporation owing anyone a career is from N. R. Kleinfield, "The Downsizing of America," *New York Times,* March 4, 1996.

The plantation owners' concern that the workers, if required to exceed their quota, might stampede to the swamps is from Frederick Law Olmsted, *The Cotton Kingdom* (New York: McGraw Hill, 1984), p. 193.

Robert Reich's suggestion for tax incentives to corporations who, in summary, treat their employees fairly, is from an article by Elizabeth Kolbert and Adam Clymer, "Downsizing America," *New York Times,* March 8, 1996.

Acknowledgments

Books are rarely just the recorded energy of the author. As in the case of *Seven Simple Steps to Personal Freedom,* a book comes about because of the faith, caring and devotion of many other people. Their contributions are mostly unidentifiable on the pages while the author enjoys full credit for their labor. The contents of this book would be but my disjointed, uncollected, often unappreciated mutterings but for the vision of John Sargent, St. Martin's CEO (and my friend), who believed there was something to be said here to a wider audience than met its first release, parts of which appeared in my earlier book, *Give Me Liberty.* To him I am grateful to the marrow.

I have been so gifted with the attention and good work and enthusiasm my editor, Tim Bent, and associate editor, Julia Pastore, along with the careful, thoughtful work of my copyeditor, Paul Montazzoli, all of whom have tried to hold the anarchy of my rhetoric to some faint, diciplined line.

My agent, Peter Lampack, the best in the business, has, as usual, had his beneficent hand in this presentation in powerful and constructive ways, and the sales force and marketing people, the designers, and all who have touched this book to make it better and more accessible are in the precious part of my heart. As always, my creative energy springs from my good life with my darling Imaging who provides me love, space, and support without which I could not write a first miserable word. Without all of these angels who have labored and loved behind this effort I could have been reduced to one who thought he had something to say but who, like so many, could share it only from a soapbox on some far off street corner.

About the Author

Gerry Spence was born and educated in the small towns of Wyoming, where he has practiced law for nearly fifty years. He has spent his lifetime representing the poor, the injured, the forgotten, and the damned against what he calls "the New Slave Master," mammoth corporations and mammoth government. He has tried many nationally known cases, including the murder defense of Randy Weaver at Ruby Ridge, the Karen Silkwood case, the case against *Penthouse* magazine for Miss Wyoming, and other important criminal and civil trials. He is the founder of the Trial Lawyer's College, which has established a revolutionary method of training lawyers for the people. He is a well-known television commentator, and continues to practice law from his office in Jackson Hole.

Spence is also the author of twelve previous books, including the best seller *How to Argue and Win Every Time, From Freedom to Slavery, O. J.: The Last Word,* and *The Making of a Country Lawyer.* The author is also a noted painter, poet, and photographer.